A Rolling Stone

Evolution and the Ematomic Veil

Waldo E. Forbes

A Rolling Stone
Copyright © 2023 by Waldo E. Forbes

Sturges Publishing Company

ISBN (979-8-218-28710-8)

Printed in USA

For Julia, Katie, Sarah, Jonas, Tristan and Daniel

Table of Contents

em - a - tóm - ic

Adjective

Pertaining to any or all of the following;

1. The unavoidable gap between any word and the object it identifies.

2. The unavoidable gap between different understandings of a single word by two different people.

3. The unavoidable gap between the separate minds of two different people.

Example: "Dog" is a word. A dog is a thing. "Dog" can be an image in a person's mind. There is an ematomic gap in every attempt to have any two of those coincide perfectly. There is an ematomic dilemma in every effort to talk coherently about them. There is an ematomic veil which shrouds the whole process. The ematomic always introduces uncertainty.

Introduction

Humans have two sides to our nature which are often at war with each other: human vs. animal. Both are endlessly complex, but the animal side has only the same complexities as in every living creature. Humans are blessed with a brain which contains a mind unlike that of any other species. Our minds are always active, engaged unbidden in cognitive thinking. In the total biological package, the mind usually appears to dominate. Our animal side has close cousins in many other species.

The individual human

If one separates two imperatives, a biological one and a human one, either can completely take over, often at inconvenient times. We tend to feel that we are in complete control, but that is illusion. The processes inside each human require further inquiry because the entirety is housed within one human body. That human body is irrevocably separate from the bodies of all other beings, but obvious commonalties create a complicated mix of independence and interdependence. The existence of the ematomic gaps creates a veil which can never be fully removed from our human minds.

Survival has long been accepted as the true biological imperative, but the factors which allow that to happen certainly depend on both the human and animal sides. A certain form of trust in others seems essential, but our human tendency for self-righteousness, especially about the limitless capabilities of our own minds and the certain correctness of our own opinions and thoughts, stands in the way. Our *true* abilities seldom align with our self-perceived abilities. Ego puts on blinders, and prevents us from being even-handed towards the equally justifiable self-righteousness of our neighbors.

Self-righteousness

We do little to build reliable tools for evaluating the quality of thoughts and opinions, either those of ourselves or of our countless neighbors. Most of human history has been devoted to establishing elaborate networks of elites to do the thinking and the evaluating. Simultaneously , we rely on, yet distrust, the very networks which we have created. Our greatest unrecognized barrier is a failure to recognize the existence and role of the ematomic; it makes the entirety of any human network precarious.

Self-righteousness closes minds. If we hope to come to understand the viewpoint of another human, we must open our minds to jointly identify a set of facts upon which we can agree. The facts can then become a basis for a set of rules which can lead to actual conversation.

Human rules

Rules for conversation are essential. Without rules, our animal side, reliant only on power and survival, will always prevail. Rules for productive interaction are a human construct. They can only be agreed upon after thought and debate. Any human, as opposed to animal, contribution to both individual and collective survival depends on the application of and adherence to rules.

Ends vs. means

Collective survival is often at odds with individual survival. For animals, the ends *always* justify the means. For humans, the ability to think opens up choices. For responsible humans, the ends never justify the means, a fact which should be a mantra for all of us. Even in matters where there is complete disagreement, it ought to be agreed that the ends never justify the means to achieve any chosen end. We must also recognize that, as cognitive beings, we always have choices. The ability to think and choose always allows us to continue to explore and come up with better means to achieve any end. It allows us to put aside self-righteousness.

Choices

Choices are simply the tools the mind gives us to assess and price risk. Risk is the trade-off between ends and means. The choices for an animal are instinctive and are rooted in survival. His risk is failure to survive. For thinking beings, the assessment can be as complex as we like, and the price based on multiple metrics. The metrics can include dollars, but it is narrow-minded and self-defeating to neglect pleasure, perceived comfort and future unquantifiable benefits.

If, whether due to laziness or cognition, our choice in any instance is that the ends *do* justify the means, we have reduced ourselves to purely animal behavior. We have decided that the risk of constructive thinking and dialog in order to better inform a choice, carries a greater price than we are willing to pay. We resort to animal power to force another into acquiescence.

This book examines these ideas. It is a speculative inquiry which tries to rely on the tools of both science and philosophy. Those tools and rules require that the starting premises of the author be clearly stated and understood, a rule which is seldom honored in practice. The rules also require that propositions be 'proven.' Proof is always a risky and controversial undertaking, with disagreements generally devolving into semantics. A better model is the legal world where there are two explicit standards. One is a 'preponderance of evidence' standard, and the second, 'beyond a reasonable doubt.' The decisions in both cases are left to humans. For this book, the reader can apply either standard or neither.

Premises

The best way to disprove a proposition is to provide a meaningful counterexample. Second best is to show that the absence of the truth of the proposition leads to an absurd result. But ultimately, the question of proof does lie in the hands of the reader to decide the matter.

In an earlier book, *A Tree in the Woods*, I defined the word 'ematomic,' and explained how ematomic gaps are an inescapably factual feature of our world, whether we acknowledge their existence or not. The explanation was built completely from two stated premises. Premises themselves require no proof, only definitional clarity for the words used in them. Greater clarification of both the ematomic and the two premises will be my starting point. The content of this book, but relies on observations which

I believe to represent facts. While it *is* my intent that the speculation provide further factual material which leads ever closer to truth, it is *not* my intent to try to convince any unwilling or unreceptive reader.

In *A Tree in the Woods*, the first premise is that our world of objects in motion exists (with the four words "world", "objects," "motion" and "exists" defined in the broadest possible sense). For meaningful philosophical inquiry, there must be both observers and the observed.

The second premise is that more than one observer exists. I am one. Both of us are able to perceive using our five external senses and to think abstractly. All observers are identical in terms of any consequences which might result from the fact of their existence. Since I am human, the second observer must be identical to me in the sense of having the same general capabilities. Being human (or human-like), we are totally separate and unique beings. All observers must have the ability to express their thoughts and to convert them into actions.

Constructs

I will use an identifier for the products of abstract thought, calling them 'constructs.' 'Thoughts' might be acceptable, but has too many existent connotations.

One way of looking at the two premises is that the existent world can be divided into two mutually exclusive sets of entities: objects and constructs. Objects have a substantial nature, meaning that they have mass or energy. Their nature not only permits of motion but requires motion as part of their continual state of being. Constructs exist solely within the mind of an observer. They have no substance nor capability of motion in any meaningful sense. Consequences such as actions result from constructs, so their role is crucial in any serious look at the actualities of the world and its evolution.

The expression or communication of thoughts may take the form of objectification, for example by writing them down. But it need not. If the communication is left as verbal, the constructs escape into the ether, but remain as constructs in the brain of the originator. They do not enter the brain of the hearer unless that person decides to create a new construct which may or may not bear any resemblance to the first, the ematomic gap at work. The well-known party game of Telephone exploits this feature.

Objectification

Thoughts can lead to actions by an individual; with or without objectification. However, another person can only knowledgeably participate in that action if its precursor thought in the first party has been objectified. Two ematomic dilemmas for joint actions exist due to the mind-to-mind and the matter-to-mind gaps. If a construct remains solely as construct, all resultant actions can only be done by the one observer, the one who has it as thought in his or her mind. Either way, actions and their effects can be perceived by any outside observer.

Objects are tied completely to the first premise, except that observers are themselves objects and can do things which lead to other objects. Constructs are bound up entirely with the premise about observers. Physical scientists study the one, necessarily using constructs, while social scientists cover the other. Other scientific inquiry and human activity is more nuanced. At their best, philosophy and theology, each with multiple branches, cover all. Regardless of how the world is studied, the two premises suffice. They are efficient and necessary starting points for all inquiry into truth about the realities of the world. *A Tree in the Woods* examined that question in depth.

In that book, I paraphrased the eminent American philosopher Wilfred Sellars. He said that the aim of philosophy is to understand 'how things hang together.' The 'how' in that phrase can be understood in both a functional and a structural way. The structural relates to the actual existent nature of things, whereas the

Structural vs functional

functional relates to the consequential effects of their existence. It is simplistic to state the obvious, that the aim of *all* human inquiry is to clarify 'how things hang together.' That truism misses the point entirely. Other than philosophy and religion, the aim of inquiry is towards specific, particularized 'things,' not a totality of generalized ones.

All philosophical inquiry that I know of has been directed at the functional 'how,' leaving the structural questions to scientists. Theological inquiry has been more broad-based, but generally constrained in other limiting ways. Theological study often gets morphed into religious study. Both religionists and theologians are notoriously poor at stating premises.

As my earlier book pointed out, there is a structural factor, namely the existence of the ematomic gaps, which is fundamental for understanding how things actually hang together. That book, while complete and capable of standing or falling on its own merits, has the limitation that it really addresses only the first premise. The study was facilitated by reducing time to its structural essence, a simple Now, as pointed out by Augustine.

Forces

Once time is reduced to a simple 'now,' notions about 'objects' lend themselves to relatively clear proof. While each object is unique, once the time factor (motion) is removed, collectively objects lend themselves to a static form of analysis. Motion, albeit present, is not a factor with a simple static now. That sleight of hand then allows an easy transition into the common terminology of the physical sciences, namely 'forces.'

There must be a "that which keeps objects apart from one another," else there could not be 'objects.' Also, there must be a "that which keeps objects together," else there could be neither 'motion' nor a 'world.' Those two "that which's" are what science calls 'forces.' The world, and most especially motion, are analog, but the removal of time converts both to the static. The holy grail of science is a single unified field theory, much as Einstein's expanded theory of general relativity was an earlier holy grail. In its time, it resolved many extremely difficult problems.

The second premise deals with observers. Singly, they lend themselves to the same type of static analysis as the objects in the first premise. But the premise states that there must be two of them! The presence of two makes everything analog, with continual motion and action. Static analysis goes out the window. Even thinking about time as a 'now' is at odds with how brains, senses and actions work. Established facts remain true, including facts about the ematomic gaps, about the unprovability of God's existence, about the finite nature of objects. Those facts stand on their own merits. But abstract thought and constructs, plus the ability to observe and to sense, to communicate and to act, are all inherently analog.

Observers

Observers have the ability to act. If we confine our study to the structural part of how things hang together, consideration of actions can be focussed on their impact on evolution. 'Evolution' is shorthand for the effects of actions by observers over time. If actions don't impact change, then they really are of no consequence.

This book will investigate the structural features of observers and their constructs in an unconventional way which I believe will prove to be informative. The book is a speculative inquiry, largely because details in the field of biology are outside my expertise. So the question of what constitutes 'proof' will lie even more firmly in the hands of the reader.

A question comes to mind which surely must occur to everyone. The existence of 'physical forces' arose immediately from the first premise. Are there additional 'forces' which relate strictly to the second premise?

Might it be fruitful to consider the possibility? My answer is a decided "yes." Much of this book will be devoted to that pursuit. By keeping the focus on the structural, I think we can find inclusive and convincing answers.

Humans vs AI

Must the observers be humans? In the first book, I left open the possibility that new creations or discoveries might enlarge the set of observers. Artificial intelligence ("AI") has a great deal of currency right now, and generates a great deal of hard currency as well. AI exists *solely* by human action, however multifaceted its layers and uses turn out to be. Unless or until there is something which pierces the ematomic veil, I do not see any possibility that the pool of potential observers will be enlarged by any human action. Such is true of basic AI, which has been around for a long time, or 'generative' or 'regenerative' AI which are the current buzzwords. If the phrase can legitimately become 'creative AI,' then the discussion might take a different turn. For legitimacy, such wording would require that the human nexus cease. Creativity is an important concept which probably merits further discussion.

A factual God

In addition to the factual existence of ematomic gaps, it was proven in the first book that the existence of God can neither be proven nor disproven. For clarification, in order to have any usefulness, 'God' must possess four characteristics: permanence, knowledge, power and omnipresence, all of which suggest an intimate connection with the infinite. An immediate consequence of the first premise is that the number of objects present in the world is finite, ruling out a God with such requisite powers. But the premise does not rule out the possibility of a God that is not an object. Nor the possibility of a God who resides neither inside the world nor among the set of objects in motion which constitute the world.

It is worth repeating here the observation by A.L. Huxley, that facts remain facts, whether or not we perceive or know or accept those facts. The facts proven in the first book were based on a discussion of the first premise and the forces arising from the fact of a world consisting of objects and motion. There are other 'facts' too numerous to mention that we can agree on (e.g. the sun came up this morning).

It is worth remembering Huxley's admonition as we consider the second premise in more depth. It is also worth remembering that we *do* have a choice. We need to assess and price the risk of either accepting a fact as a fact, or to fail to do so. Neither choice changes the nature of the fact, only the nature of the personal and collective risk we face, with potential costs or benefits either way

One aspect of the first premise which was discussed in my earlier book was the nature of human evolution. Darwinian theory is a fact. In this book, I will sometimes amend the phrase, referring to it as the biological imperative. As suggested in *A Tree in the Woods*, there are other forms of evolution which result from human actions. The instinct for survival, i.e. the biological imperative, deals strictly with the evolution of living things. It begs the question of what constitutes an 'instinct' and why? Notions about additional forces will also give greater clarity about instincts.

This book is a companion to *A Tree in the Woods*, rather than a standalone piece. Intending such, I will use much of the same terminology, plus concepts taken from the first book. The perspective is totally different, as is the purpose. The subject matter does not allow use of what science normally considers proof. My intent is to suggest questions and to propose possible answers. All of my suggestions could be considered to be propositions.

My two earlier suggestions for readers are available. If you, the reader, disagree with a proposition, show that my arguments lead to an absurdity. Or give a substantive counter-example.

Daniel and Peter

The dialog approach will be put aside in favor of a more expository presentation. With two characters, one will serve mostly as teacher and questioner. As student, Daniel has the inquisitive mind of the young, eagerly searching for new things to fill up the vessel which is his mind but not necessarily knowing which questions to ask. Peter is more seasoned. He will lay out a point of view, doing his best to suggest a cohesive and comprehensive framework for any propositions. As a case study of an older mind at work, he struggles at times to kccp track of an overabundance of accumulated information.

In order to avoid too much duplication, a great deal of the material in this introduction will be used in the following pages, often without explicit reference. Consider this introduction as an outline of the material. Hopefully it will provide a rationale for the choice of topics and processes. It will be an ongoing struggle for both the author and the reader to keep their eyes on the framework. The objective is to identify structural factors which allow observers to function as observers.

A world of objects in motion exists. More than one "human" observer exists. I am one. Let us see where those two premises lead. This book will is mostly about the second premise, the one about observers. Let us seek to better understand the *ematomic*. Our ability to differentiate perception from reality and to wade through layers of potential illusion hangs in the balance. Perhaps we can use the implications of the material in these two books to bridge some of the many gaps which divide us, some ematomic, some intentional, some unintentional.

A second personal epiphany herein? Yes. Another honest search? Yes. The reader can assess and price the risks without further help from me. Another book will not be forthcoming for assistance.

W. E. F.

After School, at the Farm

DANIEL: It is such fun to be out here. I really like all the animals. We are studying dinosaurs in school.

PETER: I've been around animals all of my life. I feel that I've learned a few things from them and about them. In many ways they are much simpler than people, but still, their complexity is amazing. It seems miraculous that there can be so much variety among living things. I learned something about living things in school, but I've learned far more on the farm by just observing their behaviors. Our senses can mislead, and we all interpret in different ways. Years of experience is a good teacher.

Animals

For example, your aunt thinks that her horses and dogs are really intelligent, and even smarter than most people. Does that mean that they can think in the same way that humans do? Is intelligence the same thing in a horse or dog as it is in a person? Probably not. We are so limited in the number of words we have to express ideas that it takes effort to see whether or not we have the same or even a similar idea in our heads. The problem is part of the ematomic dilemma which you and I talked about.

Think about your little sister who can't even talk yet. She's probably just as smart as you are but just hasn't yet learned as many things as you. She has no way to even tell you what she is thinking. But it is a mistake to assume she is not thinking. You can train your dog to do things, but good luck with trying to train your sister. Even if you can train her now, you certainly won't be able to in a few years.

A horse or a dog will watch you and take cues about what you want him to do from watching you. He'll take cues from the tone of your voice, from your facial expressions, from how you move. But if you just holler at him from the next room to get your slippers, he won't have a clue what you're talking about unless you've specifically shown him that response a hundred times. Even then, if you change the way the way you tell him what you want, or the wording, he may happily bring you something else or simply be confused. He may be smart, but he does not have the ability to think. He can add continually to the number of things he can do. But he isn't doing any of them by creating a construct, which is what a human would do. Because of the human ability to create constructs, we can and must mostly train ourselves.

If you go through exactly the same exercise with your sister when she gets older, she'll go through an elaborate thinking process to find you exactly the right slippers. She has the ability to think about what you want and to find it quite creatively. For the same reason, she will be much harder to train reliably than your dog is. While she is still quite young, perhaps before her ability to think is fully developed, she'll go along. But before too long, she will start to argue with you saying, "Wait a minute—I'm busy." But she can store the thought about what you want and can easily do it later. Your dog has no ability to store the command and do it later. It is either now or never.

"Thinking" in animals

Horses are quite similar. We are so used to our own natural ability to think that it is an automatic but non-thinking assumption that horses and dogs are doing the same thing. They do not and cannot. They cannot take things they see or hear, process them and save the result for later use. Their brain doesn't allow it. Their actions are immediate and based on the direct receptions of their senses. They do not have thoughts that they can share with others. Animals can, and do, develop an intimate relationship with humans. They can, and do, differentiate the persons who feed them and care for them and give them loving feel-good responses. But all of their actions are instinctive or reflexive, not cognitive. It is purely the human mind, inadvertently misplacing our own capabilities onto certain animals, that leads us to think otherwise.   Animal behaviors and actions are wholly based on their instinct for survival.

One thing a dog will do instinctively is to hide away a bone (for future use).   And he may or may not later remember precisely where he put it.   But instincts, not cognitive thought, will tell him that it is somewhere near. Or he may have discovered buried bones or other edibles previously, so he will dig around endlessly.   If he finds a pretty red rock while digging, a matter which would give endless excitement to a child, the dog won't happily bring it to you unless he has been rewarded by you in the past for such behavior.   And even if you reward him, he won't go around your yard and dig for red rocks!   He can indeed be *trained* to do just that—a difficult training job to be sure.   In contrast, a child, who can think, can be *encouraged*, not trained, to do exactly the same thing.

We would never waste time training a child for such a simple thing, but we spend hours training horses and dogs to do simple things that a child might do just by being asked or encouraged.   The child may choose to do so or not, assessing the risk/reward.   If offered a piece of candy as incentive, the child will dart off immediately.   If you offer a piece of candy to the dog, he will happily gobble it down and look for more, not a good idea with candy.

"Thinking" in humans

Other species such as dolphins and crows come to mind as ones some have claimed to possess the ability to think abstractly.   But deeper analysis of the elements truly requisite for abstract thinking put the lie to such claims. Thinking really is a uniquely human ability.   Survival is a complex process so it is easy to get distracted as one considers thoughtful cognitive behavior versus instinctive or reflexive behavior.   And some species or individuals are so easily trained that the distinction gets blurred.

There is a followup question: after millennia of animal evolution, how and why can it be that only one species has developed the ability to think abstractly?

Evidence suggests that, among the early versions of humans, such as *Homo sapiens, Neanderthals, Homo floresiensis* and *Denisovans,* not to mention even earlier humanoids, only *Homo sapiens* acquired the ability to think. And pretty recently. The survival advantage is enormous. Why has the ability to think abstractly not developed in other humanoid or even non-humanoid animals? It is not as simple as cranial capacity. And human brain structure seems similar in other ways to that of other species.

Homo sapiens

Consider the overview. The evolutionary process to create multiple humanoid species took hundreds of thousands of years. Once the ability to think started in just one of those, *Homo sapiens,* the elimination of all others took place in only tens of thousands of years, perhaps less. We don't really have clear evidence of the first ability to think. The Bible, based on oral history, suggests four to five thousand years ago. Oral history is not possible without the ability to think and to communicate, our requirements for an observer. These matters precede records. They don't allow replication, so we can only speculate. In contrast, instincts have been honed by millions of years of evolution. They are based on the biological imperative to survive, first as an individual, and thereby, as a species. There is no thinking involved in the working of instincts.

A survival force

The question arises as to what might be involved in this evolutionary process. The instinct for survival appears to have all the characteristics of a force. It appears structural as well. Actions are taken by living things in the interests of their own individual and collective survival. The actions suggest a "that which" causes animals to try to survive, which is precisely what defines a 'force.' Actions are the result of the presence of a force, but are not the force itself. The force operates within the brains of living things in predictable ways. The manner of operating somehow differs in a cognitive brain from that which occurs in a reflexive brain. The instincts of the latter are wholly directed at survival, whereas in the brain of a human, either cognitive or reflexive actions can result. The cognitive ones can be directed towards collective as well as individual survival. Forces are only describable by the behaviors they lead to, as are the forces which affect objects and motion. The time-scales of evolution don't allow experimentation, but even in a petri dish, the operation of a force for survival seems evident without any leap of faith. Mice and fruit flies seem to show that such a force is at work.

The existence of another force seems equally clear, the force of life itself. The instinct for survival is transmitted in the DNA of multitudes of living creatures. It leads to some living and some dying. The force of life itself is an individual phenomenon, the will to live. All living things have a will to live based on survival, but it seems stronger in humans. The presence of a cognitive brain must be able to increase the intensity of the force. It also seems to have a connection to the natural aging process, and seems distinct from the survival instinct.

A living force

To be structural, capability for the force would need to be transmitted in some manner by DNA. Otherwise, it would start afresh in each newborn and have no generational carryover. It seems similar to what happens with constructs: the DNA carries the capability for the force to exist, but the actual operation leading to actions is specific to each new individual. No organism having the capabilities we have discussed has been created from non-living material, despite extensive knowledge about DNA. Nor does such success seem to be on the horizon.

The presence and nature of these forces may well be the limiting factor in our ability to duplicate life. We might put together the pieces of a mouse, but how does one get one's hands on what is needed for the mouse to have the will and instinct to live? The forces relating to objects and motion are simple, but still lead to a chicken or egg question: which came first, the objects/motion or the apparently resultant forces? It all happened out of nothingness. Historically, both did happen, but evolution, not creation, is the subject of this inquiry.

A structural look at how things hang together starts with study of what *is* and what keeps it that way, not how it came into being. We can identify existent forces, but their actual creation may be out of reach because of the overwhelming complexity. Living material complicates the matter even more. A true understanding of what a force actually is may be beyond our grasp since we can only look at resultant behaviors.

A procreational force

Another force is crucial as part of the biological imperative to survive. It is the drive to procreate. This force must exist for perpetuation of any living species. It is a structural necessity. In humans, it takes the form of the sexual urge which may include side effects such as modesty, exhibitionism, etc., all of which relate to the need for communication between observers. It's intensity rivals and can even exceed the will of an individual to live. It is present in every living entity, each of which is unique, with a unique configuration of structural detail. Insofar as the structure is determined by DNA and not by the environment, it and the resultant force will continue to be transmitted via the DNA.

All of the parts of every living entity are heavily interconnected, so the forces operating inside them must be as well. Although the center for the forces is in the brain, there are mutual dependencies and internal communication mechanisms which may be themselves differentiated in the DNA. The flow of chemicals in humans and many other species, as well as the genes themselves, have created two sexes.

The procreational force seems mostly independent of the structural differences, but the ovulation cycle clearly affects it. The existence of the force legitimately brings into focus the general notion of equality. What does the word "equality" actually mean? It is worth repeating much of what as said in *A Tree in the Woods*. I discussed the concept of hierarchy which is the parent of equality. In our world of objects there can be no such thing as either hierarchy or equality because each object is unique. And unique means inherently different The notions of equality and hierarchy are human constructs, without any possibility of reality in the actual world. The existence of forces allows there to be functional equality. But even functional equality is very hard to identify unless the matter can be reduced to mathematical formulae, which are also human constructs.

Equality and hierarchy

Differences are a fact, but are not hierarchical. There is no such thing as any natural order. Both the survival force and the procreational force create winners and losers. One can look at evolution as a hierarchy, but that as a corruption of the word, and a corruption which introduces the notion that the world is headed somewhere identifiable. While those are logical speculations, they are beside the point. All objects are unique. Occasional physical or behavioral similarities only distract from that underlying fact. It is more productive to recognize and honor the differences, seeking only common behaviors.

Scientists create endless categories using a similarity of attributes. For serious philosophical inquiry into how disparate things hang together, be they objects or observers, that scientific approach obscures the value of the uniqueness. It is more relevant that the procreational force seems closely related to the kinetic energy of objects, being a force just waiting for expression.

When we consider the notion of forces in the context of living things, there is a special difficulty. When the forces are physical ones between objects, there are common characteristics like mass and speed for which useful measures can be devised. One can isolate forces and talk meaningfully about equal and opposite forces.

Static terminology can be used. But the structural forces in living objects have a fluidity and interconnectedness which makes any simple approach untenable. One cannot isolate internal forces from physical ones which result from actions taken by the objects themselves.

Human study

My observations on the farm suggest that, even though similar forces exists in all living things, some are measurably stronger in humans. Does the thinking nature of human beings provide an extra power? It does permit the channeling of forces into actions, and those actions can easily impact other forces, a functional result from the structural ability to act. Experimentation or analysis to separate these factors is impossible, although I believe there is a great deal which purports to do just that. With humans, most analysis would be a statistical after-the-fact study of groups and individuals, for ethical and practical reasons. But detecting details about force differences requires the powerful micro-tools available to physicists.

Before moving on to why the existence of potential forces matters for the nature of observers, one additional observation is needed. What other behaviors are uniquely human and appear to be structural? We seem to be by far the most ready to kill others of our own species. This behavior might be either because of or in spite of the ability to think abstractly and to make cognitive choices.

Urge to kill

I am not a biologist, but I have heard it said that rats are the only other species that kill their own. But one can argue that such killing by rats is a survival instinct, not a cognitive action such as the killing performed by humans. Finding food might be a survival concern for rats. In humans, there is a force which is related to our ability to think that drives this urge to kill. Just as other forces are influenced by other components of the human body, there are hormonal and aging factors. It is hard to identify just when the force starts to appear. It may be related in some way to the procreational force, but the intensity to actually kill a fellow human is puzzling.

A crucial factor for comparative analysis of humans versus other living things is the role of choice. Making choices is a necessary part of the biological imperative for all living things. In animals, making choices is reflexive and instinctive, but choices can either be made reflexively or cognitively by humans. We can use our brain actively, creating thoughts about how to assess and price the risks of many possible alternatives. A necessary part of the role of observers is to make choices, regardless of the values we use to establish price, values which are themselves a choice,.

Choices

To complicate matters further, observers are also observing themselves. What they see, what actions they take based on what they see, and how they communicate about the whole package, their choices are inevitably influenced by personal gain or loss, using personal and complicated metrics which are also a choice. The notion of an impartial observer makes for an easy premise but hard reality. If there is a corrective factor, it lies in the requirement for more than one observer.

Our ability to choose needs amplification. Choosing is assessing and pricing risk. Instinctively, animals do it all the time. But two factors complicate the matter for cognitive humans: the actions of other humans and the presence of counterbalancing forces. Risk and price are both subject to continual flux. But increases in either risk or price for one individual are usually simultaneous with the opposite result for others. Individual survival and collective survival can be at odds. With our brain, we can and do try to manage (reduce) risks, but that can be a fool's errand because it begs the question of *whose* risks are being reduced. The same is true of prices. For a cognitive human, the key is first, the assessment of the risks, and second, the assignment of prices which truly use the metrics which matter to that human. Two traps are common. The first is engaging in this process on behalf of others. The second is to take actions which limit the abilities of others to make their own assessments. Both are routinely done with the best of intentions, but the practice shows total disrespect for the individuality of every being.

Four forces

We have established four force-like phenomena which seem to have differentiated expression in thinking humans. I have tried to show the impact of all four on the requirements which we face as observers. In *A Tree in the Woods*, the interconnectedness of objects and motion still left gaps which created a dilemma as we tried to tie together the complete package. In the case of forces which operate inside the human brain and influence actions, the dilemma impacts evolution. Is the instinct for survival crucial for an observer, with resultant actions which change the future? How about the will to live, or the drive to procreate? What about our willingness, and even compulsion, to kill fellow humans?

A summation of the previous arguments might be productive. One purpose might be to identify and pursue a similar holy grail to that of physical scientists, a unified field theory. Perhaps the unifying concept might be the contribution of these forces to the biological imperative. There are two reasons why is hard for me to include the desire to kill on such a list. First, only humans have such a desire. Is there a biological imperative which applies specifically to humans alone? If so, it can only be due to our capability for abstract thought. We have seen that our special brains influence all of the forces. And second, the desire to kill seems at odds with the other three forces which would make up the biological imperative. Since it's aim is *destroy* humans as a species, best to leave it for now as an aberrant force. Perhaps there is room for such an outlier in a better overview.

As a counter-thought to the latter, it seems clear that *Homo sapiens* probably killed off all other humanoid beings, establishing the enduring primacy of itself as the only human species. Which came first, the desire to kill, or the capability for doing so? Mass killing is not easy to accomplish. Not being a biologist, I don't know whether there have been similar occurrences in other species. Mass killings of competitors does not seem Darwinian. It is an action, so how does such a desire get propagated?

Daniel, you are studying dinosaurs. It is clear from the record that they were killed off from a cataclysmic physical event, probably a meteor strike, not an attack by woolly mammoths or fellow dinosaurs.

Leaving aside the difficulties with the desire to kill, but continuing to pursue the notion of a consolidation, there are two avenues. The drive to procreate is either the successor or the antecedent to what we generally identify as love. Just as we did with the question of whether animals can think, we can also debate whether other animals feel love in the complex sense that we mean it with humans. The question shifts to emotions in general.

Emotions

The Greeks were known for nuanced thinking, with great precision of language. They had multiple words for love. For animals, the two Greek words *storge* and *eros* are likely to apply, although we will consider *agape* and *philia* later on. *Storge* is love based on a special relationship such as mother-child. *Eros* is better known to most of us and is the drive to procreate. It may be helpful just to consider how the forces work in humans, leaving unresolved the larger questions of operation in other species. Emotions may be more complicated there. My experience tells me that I see fear in animals all the time. Fear and *storge* seem closely related and necessary parts of any biological imperative for many species. The capability for other feelings is less clear.

Pursuing consolidation leads us to consider whether, as a force, the drive to procreate, with its adjunct feeling of love, is not just a specific manifestation of a general ability to have very intense emotions. If the force is just an example of an emotional capability, then the desire and willingness to kill fellow humans comes into clearer focus. If we can love, then we can hate as well. Other species may be unable to do either, at least not cognitively.

The separation of human from animal capabilities is made clearer as well. The drive to procreate and the survival instinct make up the biological imperative. Emotions are something else. Emotional capability, as we observe it in humans, can be either cognitive or instinctive. Cognitive emotions would be tied closely to the ability to have abstract thoughts, to create constructs, to communicate and to take actions. In a nutshell, an emotional force does operate in observers. Animals show many of the same behaviors instinctively.

I identified the will to live as an especially human force. Since it ebbs and flows as a part of the aging process, it may not be essential for observers. These collected thoughts leave me unwilling to find a "human" biological imperative.

We will now focus on the separated forces, a better route for examining structural factors within the premise about observers. Whatever the number of forces, all of them will necessarily impact other forces in a cognitively enabled way in humans. If we set aside our inclination to consolidate, it will simplify comparisons, discussions and interactions.

The fact that only humans can be observers comes into clearer focus. I have proposed four operative forces: the survival instinct; related to it, the urge for sex; the will to live; and the possession of emotions. I think that there are additional structural forces at work in us as we try to understand the full consequences of the second premise.

But perhaps it is time for a break?

DANIEL: I agree! And I am really thirsty.

Social Life, in Animals and People

DANIEL: I feel better, but you have my head spinning.

PETER: Don't ever let your brain slow down, and keep looking at these animals around us. Most of the ones we see are called domesticated animals, so think about what that might mean. Here are some of my thoughts.

Let's start from the beginning. Similar to many animals, man is a social creature, meaning that he likes to be around others of his species. Whether such has always been true is hard to determine, either from any archeological records or otherwise. But mostly because it is not an area I know much about. DNA requires that each animal come into being individually. Each starts from a single cell which must be present in an individual mother,. The whereabouts of the father can be unclear. So there must be a grouping of at least two at the beginning, mother and child. A biological fact. There are animals and other living things that lay their eggs or plant seeds and abandon those to their fate—not possible with humans. If a being is created and develops entirely ex-utero from the single cell stage, perhaps such a being will have no social instincts, but I have my doubts.

In referring to any grouping of more than one, the Greek word *polis* directs thought in the direction I wish to go with humans. In any such group of more than one, there are relationships that have to be sorted out from the very beginning. Social contract is the term I will use for any such relationship. It is a contract because survival of both individuals depends on it. It is instinctual. In some species, the contract only goes as far as mother-child, with the child reaching maturity and separation. For others, it is far more complicated.

Social contracts and the polis

These specific relationships cannot be part of the DNA which has no way of knowing anything about the other partner(s) to the relationships. Certain aspects of the initial relationship between mother and child might be transmitted via the umbilical cord, but those could only pertain to that one relationship. They could only become part of a future relationship with another being if they were part of a learned generality about how to deal with relationships in general. One important point is the difference between humans and other species. In a non-thinking species, the nature of social contracts tends to be uniform, whether the species has large and complex groupings, or simple ones. For humans, there has been a different evolutionary pattern. The pathway is closely connected to the ability to think and to take actions which affect the relationships.

Evolution of the polis

As a mother-child grouping of two at birth, that polis would have almost no chance of surviving for more than a few days. The biological imperative would compel any weak species into forming larger groupings. Within such groups, common DNA would suggest the likelihood of closer bonds based on blood relationship. It would seem inevitable for humans, who are weak as individuals, to move quickly into familial groups as their next form of polis. With evolution to larger groupings, an urgent priority for a thinking species would be to establish more complex social contracts to protect the survival of all. Groups which failed to use their ability to think, choose and act, to ensure group survival as well as individual survival, would quickly perish. Such evolution seems to meet all the requirements for there to be a force at work. A force creates a compulsion which is beyond the ability of the 'forced' object to resist. It would also be a matter of self-interest for the forced object not to resist.

To elaborate further, the DNA cannot and can never contain any information about the constructs which will gradually come to be created by that individual human brain. Nor can the DNA contain any information about the environment into which the new creature will find itself thrust. A force is a structural component of 'what is,' and acts on objects. But the force itself has no knowledge of or dependence on the specialized nature of the objects, even though it may depend on them for its precise operation. This force, which I would call a social imperative, exists because humans can think, the very feature which also qualifies them to be observers.

Cattle have developed a social contract in the form of a herding instinct to protect themselves from predators. But the notion that they are thinking about what they are doing, or that they are continually developing better ways to be a herd, is belied by simple observation. Yes, they will 'appoint' a single individual or two to keep an eye on the calves while they graze. But they do this reflexively, no matter the circumstances of the grazing location or context relative to predators. It is reflexive behavior, not cognitive. Humans might arrive at the same decision, but not before standing around a while discussing options. The social contract is of an entirely different nature in the two species: for one, static; for the other dynamic. A static modality leads to instantaneous, one-dimensional decisions because choices are severely limited.

A social force

Both cattle and humans can and do stampede as an emotional way of expressing fear. But humans can also be stampeded into a very thoughtful collective response to a whole variety of stimuli which cannot in any way be described as fear-inducing. Here are two examples, with more later as we continue discussion of the social force. The whole rationale of most advertising is to create at least a slow-motion stampede for some product. Or two, the perceived wisdom of an elite can be presented in such a way as to suggest the need for an urgent stampede into changed behaviors. In both cases, rational choosing is set aside in favor of a perceived greater urgency, whether caused by the elite or by the purveyor of the product to sell. Our human ability to think and to act individually is transformed into instinctive animal-like behavior. In humans, any danger to survival is likely just perception or

Stampedes

illusion, but in animals, possibly real. The ability to think gives time. In animal-like behavior, the ends transcend the means which is the true danger an absence of thought.

Domestication

What does it mean that cattle have become, or always were, domesticated animals? How does a species or part of a species become domesticated? How do such animals differ from 'wild' animals, even adopting human traits? The question is important. The process of domesticating other species represents an early but necessary event for the human polis to expand into ever larger groups. As stated above, the earliest form of the polis must have been familial groups. Humans have the ability to think and to make intentional decisions about actions, some of which affect their own evolution. An early choice would be to control factors important for survival. Food and some form of shelter would be number one since air and water are everywhere. Shelter, or the need for a safe place for a weak species to rest or live, would be the highest priority. However, one must remember that, for a mobile species, shelter is readily available. Food would move to very the top of the list.

Every species has evolved in a way that allows it to readily digest only certain things. Each species is also part of an elaborate 'food chain' involving other species. Animals usually digest organic material which is, or was recently, alive. Thanks to brains, humans have largely escaped being part of the food chain of other species. Nevertheless, they are faced with the ongoing challenge of sustaining such freedom, hence the urgency of shelter.

Evidence suggests that early humans were hunter-gatherers, meaning that they either started out as, or became, omnivores. However, the organic material which we can process easily is, or has become, quite limited. Not being a biologist, I don't know how our digestive capabilities evolved. My speculation is that gathering has always been easier for humans than hunting. However, the *results* of hunting are usually much more effective for longer-term relief of hunger. The net result favors hunting. These questions all play into the evolution of domestication. Over time, humans have domesticated a huge variety of both animals and plants. We continue to do so at an amazing rate.

As a simple definition, 'domesticate' means to bring into the home, or more generally, to bring under one's control. To control requires not only having something close enough that one can oversee it, but also requires taking a level of responsibility for that something in order to assist with and to ensure its survival, "caretaking" in a word. Since other species have also domesticated fellow species, doing so is not uniquely the province of thinking beings. But the ability to think expands and expedites the process. When the process is cognitive rather than reflexive, more elaborate results are possible. Squirrels reflexively store nuts for the winter, and dogs bury bones. But the cognitive action of actually making the supply captive, is a different matter entirely. Developing and cultivating countless varieties of apples, as humans have done, is a daunting challenge. Domestication of plants or animals is the result of many brains which can individually and collectively observe and adapt to the changing conditions and needs of the captive species.

What is the likely evolution of domestication? It must be considered in tandem with the evolution of the polis beyond the familial stage. Animals are probably easier to domesticate than plants, but domestication might well have started with either a favorite berry patch or a happenstance pet or some milk obtained from a wandering mammal. A thoughtful brain would quickly see multiple benefits of working to create an ever-larger captive supply.

The minds would also see the clear benefits of using one's fellows in the challenging enterprise. The evolution would certainly have occurred very much in parallel with the evolving social structure of the polis. In fact, in addition to the survival security attained via the growing social structure, domestication of other species seems to be the other most compelling ongoing companion.

In studying the polis, its features are fascinating, and worthy of historical analysis in their own right. But we are looking at the structural features of the social force, what effects did it have? One was to accompany and shape the polis. The externalities we see are the products of such a force, clear evidence of a force at work. A list is long: ethnicity, culture, religion, economics, leadership talent, physical abilities, etc. The social force is inherent in thinking humans and shaped the nature of every feature of the polis. Many other living things exhibit a less-developed social force, but without the impetus of a brain working in a polis, evolution stagnates. Animals did not and could not build elaborate cities.

Many factors make humans uniquely able to be the observers. The social force is one, requiring the use of a brain, plus thinking, communication and action. Humans have created and nurtured social structures, leading to relationships, contracts and perhaps even creativity itself. Domestication of food sources is but one example.

This fundamental social force can be added to the ones already discussed: the survival instinct; the urge for sex; the possession of emotions. The presence or absence of the ability to think abstractly (cognitively versus reflexively), modifies the nature of all of the other forces. The social force is no exception, lending further credence to notion of a social instinct which was where we started. It has all the characteristics of a force. There is both a thinking and a non-thinking 'version' of each force. The forces are essentially the same in all living things, but are affected by the presence or absence of a thinking brain. Collectively, they could all be called forces of nature.

The elemental herding or social instinct can be traced to the unthinking version of the other three forces. A feature of our behaviors is that we can choose, actively or passively, to revert to the purely animal side of our nature. This notion was stated in the first sentence of the introduction; humans do indeed have both a human side and an animal side. When we try to identify the forces at work in humans, qualifying them as observers, this dual nature complicates the matter. Our focus must remain on behaviors which are uniquely human. The complexity of evolving social structures is one such behavior. Neither ants nor monkeys will ever build skyscrapers or write a U.S. Constitution.

As we consider evolving social structures, we must not lose sight of their origins. The initial polis was one of two persons, then larger and ever increasing numbers. A key exhibit for the social force in humans was a need to have social contracts about how to live in relationship with others humans. The starting point was survival, not only for the individual but also for helpmates. The survival of all was critical to survival of the polis. The required social contracts could not be passed on through the DNA. They are so vital to survival that they would quickly become one of the very first jobs for the human brain. Although the contracts, especially if implicit, exist due to actions by the human brain, in order for there to be a meaningful contract, the constructs cannot remain simply as constructs. Even though thought is crucial to their creation, the results are the product of an unseen force which is at work in the entire process, a force which must help transcend the uniqueness of each individual.

Construct to contract

Communication and actions cannot be uniform across the multiplying human groupings. The evolution produced by the social force, although in parallel with that polis, quickly lost most semblance of commonality. But there may be essential features. Perhaps the first requirement for any contract to exist and then to persist, is that it must be perceived to be 'fair' to all parties. An aggrieved party will likely use any means available to

Fairness

break what it perceives as an unfair contract, by reverting to either force or subterfuge. The one choice is animal-like; the other a likely product of the human ability to think. Social contracts in other species are instinctive, and pretty simple. In such cases, neither the term 'contract' nor the concept of 'fairness' applies. Both concepts require cognition.

Early evidence　As one looks at forces, which, as we have seen, are structural, it is helpful to look at when they first appear in each individual. Babies are amazing, don't you think?. A notion of fairness is one of the earliest examples of the social force at work in human babies. The first contract is between mother and child, an astonishing one. Later, a notion of 'self' appears, which means an appreciation of others. Immediately, the idea of fairness comes on the scene. It seems universal in humans, not so in animals. The ultimate social contracts, especially in an evolving polis, are vastly more complex, but they all have their roots in their beginnings. The features of social contracts and networks evolved organically from necessity, albeit shaped heavily over time by external conditions. The human brain is wonderfully complex.

This social force is an integral and necessary part of what qualifies us to be observers: communicators and actors. An early use of the human brain, caused by pressures from the social force, must necessarily have been to shape the nature of functioning social contracts. Their generational endurance is independent of DNA. Fairness to both parties has to be the starting point of a contract or else the contract will not survive. But the notion of 'fairness' quickly becomes unbelievably complex in an expanding polis.

The essential activity of the human brain is to make cognitive choices, assessing and pricing risks on a continual basis. The existence of ematomic gaps means that we must do this activity ourselves. The essence of an ematomic gap is to introduce uncertainty, which can only be minimized within ourselves. Another person cannot possibly have adequate information about us, nor knowledge of what values we place on things, nor what we see as risks, to properly price our risks in our stead.

The most consistent failure in any evolving polis is our tendency to ignore the ematomic gaps. Whenever we try to assess and price the risks of others, there are multiple ematomic layers which preclude even the remotest chance for accurate mind-reading. Self-reliance is not a fiction but a necessity. Everything we do is done through the lens of our own separate brain. Our focus can only be to try to keep the multiple forces in balance.

Self-reliance

The polis functions as a collective, so it is easy for there to be undue distortion, usually through the socially-constructed means of money and influence, both of which usually lead to oppression of the less favored. The modality is to create a stampede, to change public opinion. The usual result is to put ends ahead of means, a simple choice which bypasses the brain and reverts into animal behavior. However good the intentions, such actions violate all notions of fairness. They can and do quickly become destructive forces for the polis itself. The polis requires the entirety to function properly.

Balance

The way in which the forces get most easily out of balance is when the values which we use to price risk and make choices get out of balance. It can be described as internal unfairness, usually driven by an overload of the emotional force. The common culprits for overvaluing are money and pleasure. The sexual urge, necessary for procreation, has today become almost entirely subverted, even for cognitive humans in a wealthy polis, into a compulsion for personal pleasure. Imbalances may or may not be self-correcting over time.

As a force, the social one would have been present in the human brain from the very moment when humans first existed. Initially, it led to the same kind of social externalities found in other animal groupings. When the ability to have abstract thoughts appeared, then the need for social contracts moved along with the evolving polis, a symbiosis driven by all of the forces in place. Early on, the combination of individual and collective survival probably dominated. Over time, with the ingenuity of the human brain to make the needed contracts, together with differing individual capabilities, the effects of imbalances likely came to dominate. The forces themselves, much like the ones governing objects and motion, must be self-correcting. We can't see the forces, only their products. Constructs such as money are what are seen, but the social and other forces are the actual evolutionary drivers. Human brains are always limited by the ematomic veil.

Self-validation

What is the structural nature of the human social force? It must differ somehow from the force at work in animals or else all would end up in the same evolutionary state. Humans have a unique craving for self-validation. Stated another way, our self-awareness leads us to know that each of us is different from every other, but leaves us not knowing what that means. Uncertainties surround us. The lack of confidence is due to the elusive nature of the ematomic gaps which are everywhere present in the real world. We can neither bridge them nor see them, but they affect us. Each introduces another uncertainty.

The craving for self-validation seems compelling everywhere, in introverts or extroverts. Unique clothing, elaborate hair colors and styles, athletic competitions, business success. If part of a survival instinct, animals do not seem to share it. Unless part of a mating ritual, their craving is to blend in with the rest of their species.

Humans also recognize that we need help on many levels from other humans. We in turn help others as part of a mutual self-validation exercise. Just as we crave validation, we can get satisfaction from validating others. All of these effects can be seen as results of the social force at work in each of us, giving us an urge to belong to an enormous social entity. It happens through the unique human brain, but is not the result of cognitive activity by those brains. The notion of a force is appropriate.

There are two primary ways we feed this validation exercise. We show a form of love covered by the Greek word *agape*, a more intense form of brotherly love. By practicing *agape*, we validate others before they actually take any action, simply by recognizing and praising them as fellow humans. Secondly, after an action is taken, we offer gratitude or thanks to validate the action and thus the person who did it. The whole sequence is how the social force works in practice. The attempt to replace *agape* by some sort of transactional alternative is what larger forms of the polis with more elaborate social contracts must do. But transactional exchanges are never as satisfying to the human brain as *agape*, pure love.

Brotherly love

Over time, in conjunction with the other four forces, incredible changes have occurred through human action in a remarkably short time. In a few thousand years, complex changes have happened for our species and to our world. It is not all Darwinian, and is more readily explained by looking to the forces in play. The changes to our actual biological makeup are quite small, with the addition of a brain capable of abstract thought being the main one. Even so, the biological evolution of *Homo sapiens* is pretty much in line with that of other animals.

Change in our world

The world itself would be largely unrecognizable to a human from a hundred years ago. The exception would be domesticated plants and animals. It is the working of the human mind which has wrought such change. It was reported recently that more than half of the surface weight of the earth has now been created by human endeavor, and most of that in the last few hundred years. Describing these effects as anything other than the work of forces seems scientifically narrow-minded. Both objects and observers have roles in the evolving nature of our world, and forces introduce a complicating wild-card.

Communication

Another requirement for observers is to be able to communicate and share their observations. In that area, evolution has been dramatic. A precise timeline is hard to establish; all animals have an ability to communicate. For humans, the key element is the need to share abstract thoughts. The elaborate structure of language arose. In a polis of two persons, language could have been very simple and likely based on using all five external senses. But as distances and numbers changed, language evolved as part of the social imperative. The objective was to bridge the ematomic gap between individual beings.

Verbal language adequate to share abstract thoughts likely coincided with the emergence and dominance of *Homo sapiens*—the selection advantages are obvious. Early pictographs and later hieroglyphs are recordings of events and other obvious perceptions of the senses such as objects. The first subject material is fellow humans, plus activities and other living things. Creation of elaborate writing for recording abstract thoughts came later. This evolution is a uniquely human activity. It is clear evidence of a force at work, demonstrating yet again the power of the human mind.

Looking at the social force, the earliest pure recordings of abstract thoughts appeared four thousand years ago with the Hammurabi code. That 'document' shows that size and complexity of an evolving polis needed much more than just verbal communications. Details about social contracts required both permanence and clarity, and hieroglyphs would not have served.

A second aspect of the social forces driving human evolution is evident in all of the early records. The recording of both objects and events shows a curiosity about the flow of time, a wish to record what is happening now so that it can be relived tomorrow. The choice is very much the operation of the human brain. Pictographs recorded observations, yes, but the brain used its unique ability for abstract thinking to see a more complex reality of time and motion. The evolution of writing had not yet reached a stage which allowed such thinking about what we call 'history' to be recorded. But the thoughts about a flow of events are there. Stories are the next writings of abstract thoughts which follow the recordings of social contracts.

Early pictographs and hieroglyphs do give evidence of abstract thinking even though they do not actually depict the thoughts. Likewise, the stories themselves give similar evidence. Their history aspect is clear, but there is compelling evidence that more was going on in the human brain. Death was omnipresent. An interest in history suggests that thinking was going on about where the collective 'we' came from, and how do we fit in with those who preceded us? I would label such thinking as spiritual speculation. This chapter deals with the social force and the ways it shapes us as observers. I'll leave the spiritual notion for later.

The presence of written language as demanded by the evolving polis brings in another complication. Humans have thoughts and generate constructs with astonishing rapidity. The static 'now' of my first book about objects and constructs is inadequate for discussing dynamic observers. Language itself quickly runs into the barrier of too few words to express too many thoughts. Since thoughts start afresh with each new observer, recorded language becomes a primary means to communicate. But it must deal with an exponential explosion of constructs. The world itself is analog, but the recorded language about it can be compressed greatly if put into digital form. The human brain has accomplished just that for recorded language. It has expanded the ability to record constructs, but has introduced ematomic caveats.

Generation of thoughts

The digital transformation is a form of translation. Two problems arise. The first is that the ematomic gaps of words themselves exist. The second is that a digital form cannot possibly contain all of the information in the analog form. But the digital format allows vastly more constructs to be objectified, exploding the information actually available to fellow humans. In the earliest polis, only direct one-to-one communication was possible. In that earlier setting, only the person-to-person ematomic gap muddled communication.

Today, there are innumerable ematomic layers between nearly all communications and interactions. The caveat about the uncertainty which accompanies each ematomic layer has been multiplied exponentially. In terms of social forces and their impact on human evolution, perhaps there is a point at which the ematomic gaps simply overwhelm the force itself, not to mention the intended communication. With the omnipresence of evolving social media, might the social force itself cease to be relevant to human evolution? Will the ematomic veil simply overwhelm evolution itself?

Observers

As noted earlier, it is risky and error-prone to undertake any serious inquiry seeking truth without stating one's premises. In *A Tree in the Woods*, I stated both necessary premises, following up with an inquiry into how things hang together. But the existence of these five forces show the folly of neglecting to point out that observers themselves are part of the things which 'hang together.' They have unique structural characteristics which cause them to hang together in a consequentially different way from other objects in motion. The forces at work suggest that a very unpredictable flux is in progress.

DANIEL: My head is still spinning, but I think I see a bit of what you are getting at.

PETER: If so, perhaps your mind is ready to consider the possibility of other forces at work? Perhaps humans as observers are even more complex than the very elaborate and confusing picture we have seen so far. But it is time for supper, so let's come back another time.

Spirituality: Reality or Illusion

DANIEL: You know, there are things which go on in my mind other than thoughts. Just last night, I was dreaming about things which seemed so real that I could touch them. But when I woke up, they were nowhere to be found. Maybe you can help me figure out what might be going on?

PETER: A very wise scientist by the name of C.J. Jung created a phrase which he came to apply to the type of effect you and everyone else might be experiencing, possibly even at the same time. It leads one to suspect that there is another side to humans, a spiritual one, working in the brain in a different way. There is a lot of evidence that humans have a spiritual side, but none that animals do. Jung labelled it the *collective unconscious*. I don't understand German, but I think that the phenomenon that he describes might permeate more of the world than just human beings. I don't believe he imposed limitations on the word 'collective' other than those implicit from the use of the word 'unconscious.'

Observers must be capable of abstract thought, with the ability to create constructs. We have not discussed whether that construction must be be done consciously. The ability to objectify constructs, which is a necessity for communication, does require that thoughts must enter the conscious, cognitive mind at some point. There is a pathway and a process for observations by the senses to become thoughts, whether or not we can identify it precisely. It happens, so it must exist.

These thoughts are speculation, partly because of my lack of knowledge, but mostly because they do not lend themselves to proof. Humans are individuals and act as individuals. I am pursuing the study of the nature of their minds by translating 'that which is leading them to communicate and to act' into the language of forces, a language more readily accessible for most readers.

Spirituality?

Earlier, I used the terminology of cognitive versus reflexive. Now I use the terminology of conscious versus unconscious, and should probably add the concept of subconscious. Extensive volumes have doubtless been written about all five of these words. I leave those for the reader to explore. I have my doubts that any of the books are premise-based, and even greater doubts that any premises have been explicitly stated. Without stated premises, it is very hard to pin down precise meaning.

My purpose with this book is to examine the nature and implications of my second premise about observers. A part of the premise says that abstract thoughts exist in observers. A structural analysis must look not only at the nature of those thoughts but also at the process which created them. Returning to the roots of the premise, the definition of abstract thinking is the ability to take the output of the five external senses (observations) and process those into thoughts, communications and actions. So far, we have looked at the nature of the thoughts themselves, focusing on how those differ consequentially between humans and other living things. We have not considered the process leading to those thoughts.

The process of thinking

In earlier chapters, we have seen five forces at work in the human brain: a social force, arising out of and modifying the human polis; an instinct for survival; an urge for sex; a will to live; and a presence of emotions. A form of all five forces exists in other living things, but each has been modified consequentially by the ability of the human brain to think. I will use the catch-all wording of a spiritual force (or forces) to identify whatever might lie outside of the thoughts themselves, working on the intermediary processes.

Anything which works on the processes is likely to find itself among the actual thoughts as well. My choice of the word 'spiritual' may be a poor one. For most readers, their own thoughts will leap to their own preconceived definition which probably focusses on the source rather than the processes. But a word like 'extra-cognitive' seems unduly cumbersome and has its own baggage. There are other things which lie outside the cognitive but which no one would consider appropriate as part of 'the spiritual side of human beings.' Creating a new word, as I did for the ematomic, is equally inappropriate because there is nothing factual to prove.

So speculating about spirituality as part of the human makeup is where we will go. Might there be a spiritual force uniquely at work in humans as opposed to other living things? So far, the uniquely human attributes we have looked at are both rational and cognitive, even though caused by forces which are not. We uncovered the five forces by looking at human behaviors. Now we are looking for uniquely human behaviors which are neither rational nor cognitive. They cannot favor survival nor procreation nor an emotional cocoon, forces we have already described. Any relationship with the forces which we have previously discussed, or with enhancing the polis, must be incidental, not causative.

Two brilliant and widely respected scientists have written lucidly about some of these behaviors. Both look at the behaviors with a different objective than mine. *The Moral Law* They seek an answer to the question of whether God exists, using human behaviors as evidence. In *Mere Christianity* and other writings, C.S. Lewis, who might be called a philosopher as much as a scientist, identifies what he calls the "Moral Law" at work in humans. In *The Language of God*, F.S. Collins reiterates and amplifies Lewis. They refer to an innate human sense of 'right behavior.' The precise details differ from person to person, from situation to situation, from polis to polis. But the sense itself is always present, innate in humans. In my earlier discussion of the notion of fairness which is closely related. But the sense of fairness is cognitive.

This book is a litany of speculations. Whether or not I agree with the conclusions about God, whose existence cannot be proven in any scientific way, as I showed in *A Tree in the Woods*, my intent now is different. I seek structural factors which affect the role of humans as observers. But the behaviors they cite are instructive. They form the basis for my own conclusions about a spiritual force.

I see the same compelling evidence that Collins and Lewis did for the factual existence of the Moral Law, an innate sense of right and wrong, go good behavior. It is a structural fcature in our world which is far more likely true than not. Additionally, humans routinely do altruistic acts which defy rational explanation. Both Collins and Lewis explain the matter far better than I ever could. It would serve no purpose to give either examples or further explanation. Behaviors occur all the time which show the existence of both altruism and the Moral Law.

A spiritual force

Lewis and Collins both have a slightly different objective from my own. They seek a specific something as causative of the behaviors, leaving out the possibility that it is the human brain itself which is causative. They find one in God, and don't look beyond that focus, having preconceived notions about the nature of God. The difference may be simply semantic but I think it goes deeper than that. If the Moral Law is an exhibit for a *force* inside the human brain, it can be separated from the implications of the words 'moral' and 'law.' There is no need for an agent to be involved in its operation. A force is defined simply by its behavioral results. Such a force would fall into the category I have left open for a spiritual force, operating inside humans without either rational or cognitive action.

Forces differ from laws. Even though we talk about the Law of Gravity when we consider objects and motion, what is really of interest is the *force* of gravity, not its mathematical formulation. The scientist in both Collins and Lewis probably led them to their word choice, combined with a wish to direct minds towards the Ten

Commandments, legitimate laws with an agent. They probably were also paying homage to earlier philosophers such as Kant and Hobbes. In our case, the word 'law' directs the mind in the wrong direction. It encourages us to seek out both an entity or agent that created the law as well as the precise terminology of the law. My interest is in looking at the structural nature of the force and at its evolutionary consequences. Forces aren't identified by words but rather by their impacts.

Altruistic behaviors are uniquely human and cannot be traced to the five forces we have already identified. We simply do things out of the goodness of our hearts. Those actions are not a result of rational or cognitive thought. As Collins points out, the failure to perform an altruistic act when warranted, can lead to emotional distress. Effectively, he gives a classic example of how the different forces at work in humans affect each other.

As Collins also points out, altruism is not the only manifestation of the Moral Law. An innate sense of good and evil, of right and wrong, or morality itself, is part of our human makeup. Some philosophers now argue that morality is relative, not absolute. It makes no difference once the Moral Law is understood as a spiritual force present in all humans. *All* forces are relative. They apply differentially based on the particular situation in which they operate. The Law of Gravity has the absolute precision of any mathematical expression. Operationally, the force of gravity is dependent on a particular situation.

Relativity

Even Einstein's famous equation is absolute, but it is put into practice via his equally famous theories of relativity. He moved beyond the notion of a force as an invisible 'thing.' He pursued the only possible course in studying forces. Just as Newton had done before him, he described what the force does functionally, letting that be what the force 'is.' Operationally gravity affects the very nature of the whole space time-curvature in which we live, a matter which needs further clarification. In *A Tree in the Woods*, I removed considerations about our world as a space-time curvature simply by reducing time to a 'now.' When we deal only with objects and motion, using ourselves as static observers, such a choice is valid. As we look at observers themselves, we do not have that luxury. Observers can only be considered in a dynamic way, which introduces the difficulties discussed earlier.

Einstein used constructs, i.e. mathematics, to discuss forces, a similar sleight of hand. That choice, a necessary one, leads into the ematomic dilemmas and uncertainties described in my earlier book. Subterfuges can help to clarify. In a dynamic world, there are no such things as 'objects' in a sense with which a very precise Einstein could agree. There are forces. He might fault my choice of wording, but I don't think that he would disagree with either of my premises. It would be fascinating to know how he might state his own premises. I will leave it for others to state alternate premises which might supersede mine as a starting point for describing the existent world.

Perceived behaviors

It is time to return to discussion of the spiritual force. Other living things do not seem to have any sense of right or wrong. They are guided by a survival instinct and other impulses. If we think that we see such behavior, it is only in domestic animals. By their long association with humans, at times they can seem very human-like. As discussed earlier, we are so unique as individual humans that it can be hard to distinguish actual behaviors from our perception of those behaviors. It is also very hard to design experiments to detect the nuances of many behaviors, either in animals or in humans.

The matter of altruism seems much clearer. I cannot identify any altruistic behaviors in other animal species, even domesticated ones.

The question which immediately surfaces is whether there are components of the spiritual force in addition to a profound innate sense of right and wrong, plus altruistic behavior. The starting point for such a search is once again to seek behaviors which are uniquely human and are not found in other living species. It is important to remind ourselves of the definition of "spiritual," namely behaviors which are neither cognitive nor rational. They appear to surface during the process of converting observations into abstract thoughts. They do not come from the thoughts themselves nor do they come from the resultant communications and actions.

There is one such uniquely human behavior which meets the criteria. It is our propensity for excess. All other non-domesticated species, when in the wild, are self-regulating. Animals eat the right amounts of foods needed for survival, even if more is readily available. They drink the proper amounts of necessary and appropriate fluids; they get the right amounts of both rest and exercise. It can be argued that such behavior is necessary for survival. I agree. Animals and plants regularly exist in such a manner; humans do not. If food is available we routinely eat too much. We drink too much of poorly chosen fluids. We often get too much or too little exercise or sleep. Almost everything we do, we readily and almost compulsively do to excess. Such behavior is neither rational nor cognitive since multiple negative consequences are well-known.

Excess

The force of excess operates somewhere between observations and thoughts. We see or sense something, but short-circuit the thoughts about the proper response even before the thoughts can occur. We see or smell a potato chip, and we are hungry, but really only for one. So we compulsively eat twenty or more. Such behavior is neither truly cognitive nor rational, and is properly characterized as part of how the spiritual force works. Present in humans but not in other living things, it can even disqualify some humans temporarily as observers. It can and does affect our ability to create abstract thoughts, to communicate and to act.

It is also likely to be the force which causes humans to revert to animal-like behaviors, subverting their human side, even though the force itself is not found in animals. Animals themselves, when domesticated or under the control of by humans, can tend to be subject to excess, as in eating or participating in horse racing or other 'sporting' activities. We praise our competitive spirit.

This complicated spiritual force is present in humans. Two questions remain. What is the evolutionary history of the six forces, now having been increased by one? And second, what are the implications of their existence as evolution moves forward?

The evolutionary history is structural fact and seems straightforward. The instincts for survival and for living are in our DNA. They are purely Darwinian, tweaked by the introduction of the human brain. Emotions and the urge for sex are also in our DNA, and also tweaked by the brain. However, the needs of the evolving polis, ever expanding and becoming more complex, are in dynamic synergy with the social force, likely with the brain itself. Its evolution is on a totally different and more rapid time-scale than any Darwinian one. What about spirituality?

Spiritual evolution

Earlier, I gave historical evidence for emerging and developing questions by the human mind about who we are and where might we come from. The need to put shape and substance to such thoughts is evidence of a force at work. The easy course is that these are thoughts. They evolved in the same way as all capability for abstract thought, as a consequence of the emergence of the human brain. But as thoughts, they are unique to each being and cannot be part of the DNA. Two evolutionary factors appear to be going on. The fact of a spiritual force itself is part of the DNA coding. But evolution may be a synthesis of the evolution of the DNA with the consequences of an ongoing spiritual force, consequences which happen anew in each individual. In short, the evolution of the spiritual force is complicated.

What are the consequences and implications of a spiritual force which lies outside rational and cognitive reach? Thought and reason are our tools for analysis, leaving us without the means to properly consider the matter. Since we are examining the structural factors which affect the second premise, speculation continues to be the only available method. Our inquisitive minds lead most authors quickly into unacknowledged speculations. True facts are elusive, so the 'preponderance of evidence' standard of proof is used more often than most of us like to admit. That is also how we must study spirituality.

The spiritual force drives us in two directions which seem to be in conflict with each other. One leads or pushes us towards a moral good; the other, towards excess. Both forces coincide in variously modified ways with the teachings and encouragements of all religions. In the case of moral good, both Collins and Lewis cite numerous examples of the bedrock principles of religious thinking, citing the Moral Law as a primary rationale for the existence of God. I find it helpful to start with what I mean by an existent God. To repeat, for me, God must be: omnipotent, all-knowing, eternal and omnipresent.

I have difficulty with that starting point when one discusses a spiritual force. One must look to the origins of the force, to its relationship with an evolving human and polis, and to its manifestations in behaviors. The appropriate question to ask is where have these forces taken humans in the past and where are they likely to take humankind in the future. I discussed the history of the other five forces in earlier pages. For the future, the procreative, survival and emotional forces will try to lead or push us towards continuing survival of the species, unless or until supplanted by another species.

The history of the forces

The social force is a very fast-acting wild card. The past direction of the polis has been to steadily increase in size and in complexity. Simultaneously, the tools to manage that ever-increasing complexity have always kept pace. There is no reason to suppose that our tools will ever be unable to keep up with the changing polis, no matter what form it takes. Even so, there are just as many doomsday predictors today as there have been from the beginning of time. The present ones have no better crystal balls than those of the past, no matter how extensive their credentials. All earlier ones have proven to be false prophets. Such is the likely outcome going forward as well. The forces seem to have been working towards survival of *Homo sapiens*.

The primary evolving difference, as mentioned at the end of the previous chapter, is the explosion in the number of ematomic layers influencing the communication between observers. It is the fragility of the communications link in the role of observers that poses the greatest uncertainty as we go forward. Unless we can cognitively figure out a way for the ematomic veil to somehow be lifted just a bit, the effects of the social force are hard to predict. Recognition would be a good starting point.

The duality of spirituality

The spiritual force has two prongs. The one which leads to excess has created what Christian theology calls sin, a concept which covers many other behaviors. The view that spirituality is a force springs from different roots and leads to a different way of seeing the world as it is. It would serve no purpose to try to align our look at the requirements for observers with religious worldviews. This aspect of the force will continue to operate as long as there are humans faced with excess.

Whether excess is a good or a bad thing depends on many factors. For the mixture, it is generally true that excess in one part of the polis leads to, and may even cause, deficiencies elsewhere. Christianity may teach resistance to that aspect of the spiritual force for multiple reasons. It may focus on the collective as well as the individual harm. Excess in one place is likely at odds with the notion of fairness as well.

The other prong, the force of the Moral Law, has led humans to create what they call God. Theologians, who generally start with an existent and external God, see the causality in reverse. From what we have seen about forces at work in humans, the force of spirituality defines the nature of God, not the other way around.

It is better for now that we keep our eyes on the speculations which comprise this book. All credible evidence suggests the existence of spiritual force. Forces of all types are the structural reality for both the physical world and for observers. The spiritual force is neither rational nor cognitive, but exists inside the human brain. It will cease to be when that brain ceases to be, but the force itself will exist forever, or as long as humans exist. Humans are the only observers we have been able to identify. Once observers cease to exist then neither premise has any rationale for existing!

Living vs non-living

The force has the same capabilities of any force, leading to the behaviors we have identified. It can only be described by what it does, not what it 'is.' It affects every choice made by every human being. In a sense, the existence of choices, intentional and unintentional, conscious or unconscious, are what distinguish living material from non-living material. The sum of all knowledge may not be contained in a single brain, but it is contained in the totality of all brains and what they have objectified over time

Does this notion of what comprises God resolve the general question about God's existence? Probably not. It just shifts the terms of debate onto the nature of forces, a matter that has come up before. To repeat, forces can only be defined in terms of what they do. The question of the existence of God depends on what one expects of God in terms of actions. I will leave it to readers to decide whether the forces we have identified, including others which we may uncover, satisfy the requirements they wish to see in God.

Four questions

Four questions remain for which there is neither an actual nor even a proposed answer, neither from philosophers nor scientists. Philosophers remain stumped by the ematomic dilemmas addressed in *A Tree in the Woods*, with no way to lift that ematomic veil. Scientists have no satisfactory answers, nor even plausible theories, for three basic questions. The first is how did something arise out of nothing? Every description of the Big Bang, etc., always starts with a 'something.'

The second is how did life come into being out of pure rocks, chemicals and energy (objects and motion)? Pathways have been proposed, but there is no credible evidence for any of them that I have seen. Nor have there been any productive experiments, the tools of science. Life, once started, has sustained itself uninterrupted, for millions of years, a daunting accomplishment unlikely to be duplicated, and certainly not by any experiment.

Thirdly, how did the thinking human brain come into being in only one species, successfully resisting all efforts to duplicate its capabilities?

Finally, there is the larger question of how the forces themselves, the ones in my earlier book plus those in this one, come into being. They operate flawlessly to create and sustain objects and motion. They drive the reality of human observers. In a real sense, which came first, the chicken or the egg.

DANIEL: You are making me very hungry.

PETER: I think your grandmother prepared either some fried chicken or some eggs, so let's go check it out.

Creativity: New or Recycled

DANIEL: I think I would like to do a little exploring off the farm, much as I like the animals. Grandmother's cooking is great, but there must be other places to see.

PETER: I think perhaps we should spend a little time looking around at more than just animals. I've been thinking about the process of creating constructs, one of the things we must do in order to be observers. For real communication, those must become objectified. It should be interesting to look at some results. Let's go over to my neighbor's place which is an interesting building, filled with some fascinating stuff. You might be more interested if she had some robots. But she's almost as old fashioned as I am, so I don't think you'll see AI at work.

Objectified constructs

Look at her house over there. What do you suppose led her to dream up something like that? No other living creature could come up with the idea for such a thing, let alone build it. What a showcase! Perhaps an outside force put it into her mind. But which one? My quick idea is that it is an example of her desire to be validated by others, noticed for her uniqueness as a human being. If correct, then the force would be the social force.

Due to the complex and individual nature of humans, no structural forces at work inside of observers can be translated into the language of mathematics. Some forces, such as the spiritual one, seem only to exist in humans, while the others seem to be present to some degree in all living things.

When we see others create remarkable things such as handsome buildings, there are two ways to study the process. We can use our abilities as observers, or we can try to see the construction through the eyes of the person who was inspired to have the idea for it.

As an observer of her creation, several things could happen. I might dream of doing something even grander.

The social force works in such a way. Given my lack of talent, that dream is unlikely to happen. I might simply tell her how nice it is; such a statement would validate her with my thanks for her creation, while also validating myself for my ability to notice her greatness. The social force also creates such endless circles. A third possibility might be to offer her a lot of money to buy it. Money would reinforce my thanks with cash. I might try to duplicate her creation, either in every detail or just as a model or roadmap. Those are social forces at work in me as the observer, encouraging me to take actions. They happen in me, and give me choice(s). None are choices an animal would or could make.

Creativity

The mere sight of her creation stirs in me a need to make some kind of response. Perhaps one effect of her creative process and its result is that it unleashes just such a response in multiple observers. Such unleashing is part of what happens to create the totality we have labelled as the social force. When one watches toddlers at play, one sees creativity cascade from one to the next. Animals play too, young and old, but play in itself need not be creative. Animal play is likely to be another part of the social force which is present in many species.

A function of observers is to take actions based upon a combination of observations with how the observations are processed by their brains. In the case of creativity, symbiosis is exactly what happens. Receptions by our senses trigger thoughts, leading then to unique cognitive actions, often creative and usually unpredictable. A desire to encourage just such responses is undoubtedly part of how the social force worked in her. The human brain is complex; multiple forces work in and on it

It is equally important to consider how the creative process itself works in *her*. Is it just the social force, or is there something else going on in her. Might there be a separate structural force involved? Our starting point is a description of uniquely human behaviors, the results of a force at work. The force itself is part of the structure of the observer. Is creativity as simple as an effect of another force? The social force is dependent on and interactive with the surrounding environment, primarily through the communication requirement for observers. A separate creative force might have social consequences and still be a force acting directly on her alone. My response to her creation is actually a response to the remarkable nature of her brain, and only indirectly, via the social force, to her as a person.

The action in her is the result of observations she made. Did my neighbor see something that inspired her? Did it come to her in a dream? Is it a copy of something she saw somewhere else? The human brain is so complex that any or all could have occurred. All of the processes going on in her are independent of any social force they might unleash. She might not be able to tell us precisely, and even if she did, she might be mistaken because our memory is imperfect. When you ask a child where he came up with the idea for a unique toy, which children create all the time, the child will tell you, "I don't know—I just did." One likely sequence is that my neighbor saw something that led to an abstract thought. That thought then became objectified, leading to something that we can all enjoy. No animal is capable of such behavior. The force works inside the human brain.

A creative force?

The difficulty is compounded because creativity is not wholly linked to observations, experiences or even, conversations. Where did the notions of unicorns, dragons or even purple people eaters come from. The replication in multiple forms of such ideas is easy to spot. But some human had the first occurrence of the idea, creating something out of nothingness. Yes, creativity is a real force.

In contrast, someone might say, "Isn't your word 'ematomic' a creation.?" Not at all. I was merely putting together a word to use for a very real and existent thing.

New objects, things, are discovered all the time and new names then needed to enable discussion. A better word than 'discovered' is 'uncovered.' There is no creativity in naming something which already exists, although the egos of those doing the uncovering crave validation just as much as the artist.

To belong or not to belong?

The urge for validation, combined with an urge to belong, is also complex. But these urges are not the only things which drive creativity. We want to belong, but at the same time we want to be seen for our uniqueness, i.e. for *not* belonging. The social force and the creative force intersect at the desire for self-validation. As in the case of spirituality, the dichotomy may result from brain activity on the pathway from observations to resultant abstract thoughts. There may be a feedback loop which paints the observations with a modified brush. At times, the force leads us in a consistent way, in order to enhance our belonging. At other times, the same force encourages us to do the conversion in a totally unique and new way, never before tried. This latter element is the dominant one, perhaps even universal. People, starting as children, differ greatly in their creative instincts and abilities, but all participate. The resultant variety of clothing, makeup, hair and styling choices seems endless.

All living species have senses, some less than five, but the abilities and sensitivities of the senses differ markedly. When Darwinian evolution is at work, the capabilities of any one sense are roughly the same for all members of a species. One species or sub-species may need a really good sense of smell to survive. For another, hearing is critical. All species develop acuity in the senses needed for survival. All species have an incredible ability to recognize others of their own species, no matter the camouflage or reduction in sensual acuity.

Humans are unique. One individual can consciously develop special acuity in a chosen sense, a process which is the very antithesis of the Darwinian one or any animal

one. And also the antithesis of any form of species-wide evolution. There must be a force at work which is available, consciously or not, to each individual. The fact that there are countless limits to the availability of this force does not belie its existence.

We can also teach ourselves to be better observers differentially in each separate sense. We can do so consciously, or it can happen in the same way as in animals, as part of the instinct to survive. Blind persons will generally develop much better hearing and smell. Otherwise, differentiated development depends on conscious choices. How does this ability relate to creativity, another chicken and egg question? If creative talent or capability is present at some level in everyone, how and why does it get realized? It has been said that, when an individual has an especially remarkable talent in some area, time slows to a crawl for them when they exhibit that talent. That description is another way of characterizing a very acutely trained sense, doubtless honed by years of training and focus.

Training

Our neighbor likely has a very good visual sense, and your grandmother, a wonderful sense of taste and smell. It helps her come up with some very fine dishes. I think that, even though she may be following the same recipe every time, it turns out to be slightly different each time. That is part of the creative process, and part of the ematomic dilemma which I cited in *A Tree in the Woods*: it is impossible to precisely duplicate anything if for no other reason than because it is modified a bit by the knowledge of the previous attempt. Animals duplicate, humans cannot. For their own satisfaction, people try to do everything slightly better than they did before. Internally, we must validate ourselves to ourselves, as well as to craving validation by others. We do so cognitively, continually challenging ourselves.

An ironic feature of the multiple forces which drive humans is the complexity of their interactions. There is

no way to isolate a single force to allow conclusive study. These forces are structural, but the structure is complex; it works its magic within each individual brain. It does so in unique ways in each separate brain. The forces allow us to be observers but complicate understanding of how the process works. Even their identification and isolation might be subject to varying opinions. Others might see the matter differently. But the method is sound, to look at behaviors which can readily be seen to differ from the behaviors and abilities of other living species. Cognitive creativity is not seen in other species.

Universality

A reason one might discard creativity as a force is the question of universality. Is the force present in everyone? Childhood behaviors put the lie to that thought. Children are endlessly creative, even in situations where physical and environmental conditions seem to pose insurmountable obstacles. Adults are too, although their creativity can be more readily muted by external factors. Children do play in endlessly creative ways, period. And adults are also endlessly creative in truly astonishing ways, period.

It is hard to separate our capabilities as skillful 'observers of behaviors' from the behaviors themselves. Useful measuring sticks are not available. Creativity is exhibited in an ad hoc way in multiple areas. There might be a separate force channeling this variability. If so, such a channeling agent would likely direct all forces, including the ones discussed in *A Tree in the Woods*.

A precise structural definition of the concept of 'force' is problematic, but the language of forces is useful because it is common in scientific inquiry. Most readers have a notion of what is intended, whether or not they can themselves give a precise definition.

Our purpose here is to look at structural factors which affect the nature of observers, There is an ematomic veil which clouds our inquiry just as it did for the study of

objects and motion. The sleight-of-hand needed to try to part the curtain a bit is not as readily available as was the reduction of time to a 'now' or the conversion of forces, objects and motion into the construct of mathematical expression. Better just to recognize the ematomic veil.

When we looked at objects, we saw new objects being created all the time. But those new objects are mostly just pieces of existent objects being shuffled around. The exceptions—when energy is converted to matter, both subject to new discoveries—while possible, seem to be rare, at least compared to the number of objects in the world. A similar process may apply to the formation of constructs, but there is probably more to it. We cannot observe all atoms all of the time, so these are just speculations!

Recycled vs new

The basic process with human creativity is different, for two reasons. One reason has already been described, the human urge for validation. We recognize the new, and collectively have a very keen awareness of when something is truly new as opposed to the recycling of someone else's idea. Additionally, social contracts rely on fairness for their very existence. The polis has created elaborate structures and processes to distinguish the truly new from the recycled. There is much wailing and gnashing of teeth, plus lawsuits, when the line between new and recycled is crossed.

When we make a choice about doing something which might be considered creative, we assess and price the risks. And those risks differ dramatically dependent on the field of endeavor. If we create a dish for dinner at home or even for a party with lots of attendees, there is little risk that someone will claim that we have recycled their idea. But it does happen.

The risk increases if we wish to sell our 'new' dish in the marketplace. The risks in matters of the sense of taste are minimal because the sensation of taste is very particular to individuals, and is hard to pin down. Smell and touch face similar challenges. None of those three senses are especially acute in humans. In contrast, any creative artist who ventures into matters of sight and sound can touch very raw nerves and sensibilities.

This chapter is about creativity, so we will continue an exploration of the forces at work in the creative person. The evolution of the polis is again the starting point. Creativity is a dynamic process. Stationary stones only gather moss. At the first moment when thinking beings came into being, a social structure of some sort would have been in place. It would have been based on survival, without the complex communication needs which came along with the evolving polis. Any culture was based on survival. Just as for animals, the notion of cognitive, purposeful creativity makes no sense.

Mother and child

The most likely scenario, as before, is that creativity evolved in parallel with the polis. The polis started with the universality of a mother and child, a mother crooning to her baby as mothers must do. If there was a creative force at work in her, she would have tried to do so in imaginative ways, leading her to increasingly apply her brain in imaginative ways. The sounds of the forest might have shaped her imagination, but were unlikely to have caused her impulse. The motivation came from her child. Even though the polis does feed on itself, we are exploring the *causative* structural factors. Culture was a result, not a cause, and came into being organically with the evolution of the polis. It was not a factor in her initial creativity. Culture, in any meaningful sense, did not even exist until the polis had achieved a fair level of complexity. Culture is created by the symbiosis of multiple groupings of people, all necessarily different.

Individuality

Creativity, on the other hand, is all about individuals. The astonishing visual creativity we see from humans never ceases to amaze. Sonic creativity is the same. Accompanying the creativity of the artists, and working in parallel with it, much as a force would, is the response of listeners. The compulsion of humans to have sounds continuously bombarding their ears is obvious every day.

In contrast, animals prefer as much quiet as possible, in order the separate out the sounds which matter for their survival. They get confused in the presence of noise. Early hunters took extreme advantage of this behavior to assist them in the chase. Even though the five human senses may be quite different in other species, they play a vital role in the actions of our brains which qualify us to be observers. The differentiation between hunter and prey is important because, superficially, it may seem universal. But the cognitive creativity of the human has always far exceeded the capabilities of any animal, Over time, it has made the chase very unfair.

The evolving polis may be the major factor driving our compulsion to be bombarded by sounds. White noise can even be helpful for essential sleep. The consequence is that enormous energy and talent is devoted to creating such sounds. The validation of an appreciative audience is powerful, whatever its motive in supplying it.

Effects on others

Only recent documentation of sounds is available so it is impossible to assess the evolution of sonic creativity. Vocal chords themselves are no help; evolutionary biologists may know when they came into being, but other species have them or some functional equivalent. Equally certain is that their relevance depends just as much on the ear as sounds themselves. How sonic waves are sensed merits study. For us, it is merely part of a premise, needing no further explanation of the how.

All creativity seems to merge seamlessly with all of the other senses, suggesting a force inside the brain. Similar behaviors in other animals reinforce the notion of action by both the social and the procreative forces. But a cognitive brain is behind the variety seen in humans. Each of the astonishing variety of sounds created by humans started as a construct in some individual human brain. Each creation started at a definitive point in time in the mind of just one person. It probably achieved objectification very early on, often to allow collaboration.

Do sounds influence the role of humans as observers? They are a vital part of an entire panoply of information required to assess objects and motion. Even though we do not normally think very much about the sounds of objects, they are part of what constitutes a tree falling in the woods, whether we hear it or not. Because the many facets of our elaborate sensing apparatus are all we have to work with as we perform our role as observers, it is easy to forget that the nature of objects and motion is the reality of our world. We are merely observers, but we observe a great deal more in a greater variety of ways than we usually recognize.

The world *itself* does not depend on observers. Our relevance is only when *we* wish to discover and use truths about that world. The first premise fully describes the world. But philosophical inquiry requires a someone to figure out how *everything* about the world hangs together.

Role of the observer

We started with looking at my neighbors house. Isn't it wonderful to be blessed with these eyes. That house too started out as construct in someone's brain. And then it became objectified into the amazing thing we see here. I suspect that it changed a great deal throughout the process, from the first inkling in her brain, probably through many iterations while still there, and then during the time it was being built. Creativity is a dynamic thing, and change may well still be going on.

Perhaps the hardest part of the creative process is the decision, at some point in time, to stop and to finally objectify the constructs which continue to overflow the mind. While they remain as constructs, they can continue to evolve. The creative force does not stop, even after its products have been objectified.

In contrast, one sees a bird building a nest in a very 'creative' way. No matter how elaborate, that process is instinctive, to make a safe and nurturing place for the babies. It ends when the babies come because survival causes other priorities to replace it. There is nothing cognitive in nest-building. It is a different process than the dynamism of creativity.

The visual world has even more variety than the audible. We mentioned the role of pictographs earlier; they are a critical part of the evolution of visual creativity. The realm and role of what we might call visual art is a wonder, and is being enlarged every moment. Most artists have the same difficulty as other creative persons in making the choice to end a project. They face the same trade-off of external deadlines, which are simple, with an internal desire to make the work just a little bit better. In both music and visual art, there are countless 'unfinished' works. Some notion of 'perfection' shows the self-validation need of the artist in practice. Each individual walks that tightrope alone. Price vs. risks.

Visual creativity

Outsiders are prevented by the ematomic reality from ever 'knowing' or 'seeing' or 'hearing' the construct while still inside the mind of the artist. Varying forms of objectification are crucial to the creative process. In assessing the costs and benefits of objectifying, i.e. finishing the project, there is a struggle between the validation which can be provided by others with the need for adequate self-validation. The costs and benefits of every choice are very hard to assess and price, but doing so is an essential part of being human. None of these processes go on in other species. They also go on in very different ways in every separate human.

Language was a necessary result of the social force at work. The human creative process has transformed the reality and possibilities of language in astonishing ways. Some serve the requirements for humans to be observers, but others are purely and simply creative. Poetry, fiction,

Language

educational tomes, song lyrics and notes, the laws of a nation. Just listing the many uses for written language is an exercise in futility. Hundreds of books are published every day, with millions of other written communications abounding.

Uncertainty

There is a permanence to the written or recorded word which helps to reduce the ematomic uncertainty inescapable in the use of words themselves. But caution in looking at the number of ematomic layers is prudent. They have a way of sneaking into every aspect and means of communication without being noticed. Each one brings uncertainty with it, undercutting the vital role of communication as an essential duty of observers. They can quickly explode exponentially

I can't even begin to find enough books to satisfy you and your brothers. Some you read for yourselves, others you like to have read for you, probably because there is pleasure in the sounds of the voices reading them. Both reading and being read to can spur more creativity in you, and in different ways in your brother.

To serve as observers, simple communication is adequate. But to serve as knowledgeable participants in the entire observation process, then all of the elaborate means we have developed are useful. Perhaps this process is the clearest demonstration of the social force at work. The creative urge of humans is an integral, even if complicating, factor. The social force in animals does not even begin to reach these levels.

I think we should now take a look at possible structural ways that these creative forces impact both observers and creators. Bur for now, I am ready for a break.

DANIEL: I'll look for a creative way to get us another drink.

The Eyes of the Beholder

DANIEL: I think I made better choices.

PETER: I think you just think your choices were more imaginative. But, guess what, the ematomic veil makes your opinion just as valid as mine. Just make sure it is a reasoned opinion.

DANIEL: I have been thinking about whether I would rather have all of this stuff read to me. I'm not sure. Sometimes I can remember better what I read and sometimes what I hear. I guess one can ignore or discard either one. And sometimes I just want to go play.

PETER: A good idea. Let me give you a few thoughts about that before we go outside. I was told a long time ago that there are specific and distinct types of learning styles. I was also told that the entire subject is very controversial. The earliest ones which I learned are the visual, the auditory and the kinesthetic. Later someone told me that the visual had been subdivided into what I would now call pictorial visual versus reading/writing visual.

Learning styles

Scientists specialize in endless subdivision, and it is doubtless helpful for studies and experimentation with particularized objects. But studies involving people are problematic, due both to their uniqueness and to the ematomic veil. Each person is an individual, and each brain, the true subject of any study, is endlessly nuanced and hard to get at reliably. For the purposes of this inquiry into the second premise, one must go back to the statement and purpose of that premise rather than be distracted by the unimportant.

The premise identifies five external human senses, the receptors for all observations to be processed by the brain into abstract thoughts. These thoughts or constructs are the basis for communication and action. Precisely *how* all of this happens is a legitimate realm for scientific inquiry. For me, the relevant fact is the premise that such a process *does* happen. Premises must be self-evident and stand on their own merits. They are off-limits for further explanation. Otherwise, one gets distracted into the rabbit-hole of an endless series of "why" questions. Daniel, you know all about those. Humans, like other animals, are very inquisitive. But only humans are truly capable of asking 'why' questions.

If one feels there is a better or a more complete and explanatory answer, then simply come up with a better premise which answers a "why" in the one I chose. Premises must be necessary, sufficient and efficient in providing a complete explanation of the nature of our world. We are seeking to find out how things hang together, but the inquiry is about *our* world, not some potential other world. Reality must be our tool, and the existent structure of the world our target. This book is focussed on human observers.

Forces in the brain

The premise about those observers is the starting point. Observations come to us via five external senses. It is logical that each individual will have differing abilities in each of those senses. It also seems likely that most of those differences are transmitted through the DNA and subject to the slow Darwinian processes for change. However, the content of the human brain, its constructs, cannot be transmitted by DNA.

While there are DNA commonalties shared by all humans, the details can differ. Specific details, including internal processing, which differ from other living things, relate to the human brain. We have chosen the language of 'forces' to describe how the processes are uniquely at work in humans. Each force has its own evolutionary path, and is continually moving the evolution forward. We have identified seven forces so far: a survival force, a procreative force, the will to live, an emotional force, the social force, a spiritual force and a creative force.

In considering different learning styles, the proper starting point is the five senses, plus the forces which affect the creation of constructs and lead to our actions. Eyes, ears, touch, taste and smell: each with a pathway into the constructs we make. The constructs cannot come to us in our DNA—the only pathway for them is from our *own* observations and experiences. A child cannot create constructs involving things with which he or she has no personal experience. Even the creative force is constricted by what has been experienced. The manner of that experience and the ways in which it, and all of its fragments, enter the memory and are retained by it are very complex indeed. They are also unique to each individual. One child may experience a tiger at a very young age, another never. Such events will happen and be explained to each separate child in totally different ways, perhaps tapping into multiple senses, perhaps not. These experiences and observations become the gradually evolving material which, once present, can then be used to create constructs. At very early ages, children know a lot about what is inside their brains and what is not. They have figured out how best to add to that warehouse.

Experiences

Our constructs, even our creativity, can only be shaped in two ways: direct observation by any of our senses, or indirect learning shared with us by others. Even the sharing comes to us via the senses. First-person conversation is a better vehicle than exposition. Neither exposition nor conversation need be limited to the verbal. The important feature is that it be face-to-face, having only a single ematomic layer. Meanings can then be clarified in real time. Otherwise, multiple ematomic layers cumulatively obscure not only meanings but actual truth. Basketball players absorb more information on the fly than they do from the coach during a timeout.

The important feature of any learning style is how well the presented material is able to connect with constructs and experiences already present in the child's brain. Another way of stating the matter of learning styles is to consider how well the learner can identify and cope with the difficulties and confusion imposed by the multiple ematomic gaps.

Environment and culture

The source of the material which accumulates as information in each evolving brain can only be from the environment surrounding the brain. It must be through observations of that material and resultant conversations about it. That environment is a combination of objects intentionally placed there, with other objects which arrive by happenstance. The latter would be due to the forces described in *A Tree in the Woods,* with the remainder being the result of the forces which allow us to serve as observers.

One key feature of the polis is that, directly or indirectly, it frames the nature of these interactions, creating a resultant culture. While it does not physically create the eyes of the beholder, which are much the same for all humans, it does in fact shape how the brain processes observations, the translations of what the eyes, and other senses, see. If a child has never physically seen a tiger, then, when he does, his experience of that encounter will be as much shaped by antecedent experiences as by the event itself. Inescapably, because every person is the sum total of their experiences. That experience, for good or ill, may well have been shaped by others if there has been a determination made that the individual is a kinesthetic learner, or an auditory or a visual one, potentially narrowing irrevocably the range and nature of his abilities.

Memory

Observers can communicate and take actions, but they remain at the mercy of both present and previous observations and experiences. For *A Tree in the Woods,* the feature of memory could be ignored because time was reduced to a simple 'now.' But in the analog world of individual observers, the feature of memory must be addressed, regardless of whether or not it differs from other living things. Apparent differences seem more the result of the multitude of forces which work uniquely on or in the human brain.

Sometimes we fear offending other persons and avoid discussions about controversial topics such as learning styles. For our speculations, dialog is critical to gaining understanding in our search for truth. The ematomic veil of our words is problem enough. Avoidance is simply a choice, invoked when reversion to the animal side of our nature seems less risky than communication and discussion. We avoid talking about things all the time!

Avoidance

Our actual survival depends entirely on our ability to think. The objective of all learning, teaching and indeed, communication, should be to enhance that skill. A shorthand for all three would be conversation, any time, any place. The status of the conversants in terms of the experiences and observations filling their brains, is irrelevant. We easily forget that it is only the listening part of the conversation that can actually become new information for a participant. The communicating part merely helps to objectify existent constructs.

The limitations imposed on such things as memory and perceptions are universally recognized by every polis of any size and complexity. Social contracts depend on both memory and perceptions for functionality. But one must not lose sight of the underlying structural reality of both constructs and memory. The evolution of the human brain is Darwinian for both the size of the brain and its capabilities. Those features are transmitted via DNA.

Physical constraints

Constructs, and resultant memory of the observations and constructs, both grow at exponential rates which start very early, at some point after conception. A physically and functionally brain of limited size is asked to house an exponentially increasing number of constructs. It does not matter what the physical nature of that process is. The brain must quickly overflow. As discussed in *A Tree in the Woods*, constructs must inevitably disappear long before they have any possibility of objectification. They are truly lost forever. Neither the process itself nor the identities of the constructs which disappear matters. Supply quickly exceeding capacity is inevitable in all brains, whether the supply is simply observations as in animals or constructs as in humans. It is biological reality, no matter the course of brain evolution.

Observers

Setting aside these inevitable losses, a creative artist has total control of the materials and the fields in which he exercises his talents. But as observers of the fruits of that creation, we are limited in two ways, the first being simply access to the material, the objectified constructs. The second is that each of our own five particular senses may be unable to perceive the nuances of the creator, for all of the reasons we have just gone through.

In *The Phenomenology of Spirit*, using a functional approach, G.W.F. Hegel, goes through the entire development (evolution, if you like) of the human brain. There is a sequence going from observation to levels of abstract thought. To use my terminology, varying forces intervene in that sequence, and likely impact evolution in complex ways. I focus on the underlying structure, because cause and effect are functionally hard to separate. The relationship between the polis and resultant cultures makes it hard to look beyond the resultant features.

It is more useful to look at Hegel's analysis with an eye on two features, one being the role of forces. The second is the fact of ematomic gaps. The first ematomic gap is the simple translation of an object into a perception of that object in order to start the evolutionary sequence. Hegel identifies the gap without naming it. Once the perception is inside the brain, then constructs can be handled as Hegel does. However, constructs can be equally well be handled in other ways. Hegel's logical sequence with its rational transitions is makes a lot of sense. Rationality means dealing solely with constructs, so there could well be other alternatives. Constructs are not limited in the manner of physical objects. Likewise, they are not affected by the forces considered in *A Tree in the Woods*. Hegel does not make the distinction, either not noting it or not considering it consequential. But it is. There might be other forces which impact the dialectics he chooses. An analysis of those is for others to explore.

Forces and constructs

When observers are in their roles as observers, as unique beings, they differ from other objects. The structural forces which have the potential to affect constructs are the ones identified in these chapters. They operate differentially on each individual brain, even though their features are universal. Collectively, the forces create the uniqueness of each person and differentiate us from all other species. Each of us, as beholder, has our own set of eyes which came into being when we were born and will be forever lost when we die.

Every creator of content, who is the objectifier of that content, is also a beholder. Their content will necessarily be limited by what they have accumulated in their limited lifespan. Fortunately, their own created content has been objectified, so that part of their being can survive. The social force has driven us to create elaborate schemes to do just that. But other forces have sometimes taken us in other directions. So the question arises as to a possible hierarchy of the forces. Perhaps one can or does take precedence over the others, either at times or universally. I have already discussed the fact of the separation of our animal nature from our human nature, with our ability to make a cognitive choice about which of our natures to exercise in any particular situation.

Control over forces

Since *Homo sapiens* has survived, in contrast with other humanoid and animal species, one can reasonably argue that survival implies the existence of a hierarchy of forces. In other words, even though our brains have amazing capabilities, situations may arise where we completely lose control over one or more of the forces to another one. Implicit in such a statement is the notion that we have any control at all over the forces! That question goes back to the problem of identifying what a 'force' actually is. Forces can only be defined by their impacts, by how they work in the two premises.

The hierarchy I see occurs whenever a choice is made to revert to the animal side of our nature. The situations which arise at that point are then completely of our own making or complicity. Stampedes, plagiarism, excesses, wars and killing, etc. The list can go on.

Listeners

Our eyes as beholders allow us to make choices. The failure to recognize that one is making a choice is similar to failure to recognize one's role as a listener in a conversation. Our brain is of little use when idle. We have then abdicated our role as observers. If we wish to understand any truths about our world, we are an integral part of what makes that world by each choice we make. Our craving for validation and belonging is the most likely source of the blinders that plague us.

My earlier discussion gave reasons for certain forces to be included in any listing of structural factors which qualify humans to be observers. But as the observer, having the eyes which see, these additions relating to what and how we see, must be made for a more complete understanding of a very complex process. All of the described forces seem essential, but there might be others which I have missed.

Robots

We looked at human traits because the word 'human' was in the premise. No other living thing has those traits; a created one might. But making something with either true creative ability or spirituality seems a step too far. Creating an entity with true altruism would be daunting. It is spontaneous and relies on an innate sense of the moral law. It is incredibly difficult for thinking humans to discern and agree upon a moral good. It is hard to see a rationale for a human creator to even try to incorporate into a robot the panoply of forces we have uncovered. Yet they are all observable features of human observers.

Spirituality is special. Out natural inclination, as also for Hegel and most philosophers, is to turn our eyes towards the possibility of an existent God (Spirit for Hegel). Most who have done so have focused only on the four necessary features: omnipotent, omnipresent, all-knowing and eternal. If God is considered strictly in the context of a spiritual force, unintentional blinders have caused us to miss the most important feature of all. Our eyes, as beholders, only see in one direction. Throughout history, all observers have been totally focussed outward, toward some kind of external God.

As a force, the most likely residence for God is *inside* each and every human brain. The forces operate inside the brain. The most likely place for the kingdom of God is also inside each and every brain. Tolstoy quotes the Bible on the matter in his history of the social order, *The Kingdom of God Is Within You*. He was not seeking God. His two-fold objective was to identify the corruption over time of the social force into animal-like behaviors, and to convince readers about the power and importance of non-violence in resisting the resulting evils. He saw that the same forces, notably the social and spiritual ones, might be potential and necessary tools for a better future. As all have done, he neglected the role of the ematomic in individual and collective action. My purpose is to explore human behaviors and to uncover causes. It is up to each of us to try to lift the ematomic veil and to change our own behaviors. Multiple forces operate in us, both as observers and as participants. We are part of the toolkit for how our world evolves, but only part of it.

The nature of God

When seen from the viewpoint of forces, God does not work from the *outside in*. God resides in all humans and works from the *inside out*. The composite nature of the forces, working in unison and conflict, makes sense. Tolstoy, and later, Gandhi, as a Hindu, had much the same conception of God as other religious practitioners. In his pursuit of non-violence, Gandhi did use the term *satyagraha*, "soul force." Tolstoy felt that the resources needed for non-violence lie inside our minds. But neither revised their conception of God. My purpose has been to look at all uniquely human behaviors as the functional product of multiple forces; another view of God emerges

Our role

I have focussed on the role of a cognitive individual mind which has the ability to make choices, for good or ill, for the individual and also for a collective. As we make such choices by evaluating and pricing risks, we must place complete reliance on the one self and life we have been given. Facts remain facts, no matter our choices. Our DNA can ultimately matter or not. Our constructs can get objectified or not. Either way, we do have unlimited power over our own minds and choices.

We like to pick and choose facts to suit our narrative of the moment. I am probably as guilty of that failing as anyone else. There are two steps into any conversation. The first is to establish rules; the second is to agree on a set of facts. We tend to skip both steps, unconsciously putting the ends we desire, probably preconceived, ahead of the proper and equitable means to get there. Corrupted means necessarily lead to corrupted outcomes.

Daniel, now tell me about the gaps in what I've said.

DANIEL: My head is still spinning!

PETER: Fair enough. You have far more time than I to consider all of these matters, revising them if you choose. For me, they are now objectified constructs, and the best I can do to paint a coherent picture of our world for you.

Three choices

We can and must continually choose three things on our own, also suggested later by Tolstoy, as we try to remain clear-eyed about all of the prices and risks: the most important moment for us; the most essential person to us; and, without cease, to practice kindness and *agape*.

With extra inspiration from:

Dr. Paul Young
Hailey Helm Wiseman
Doug Goodwin
John Patton
Joan Dixon
Carol Burnes
Aaron Trembath
George Chiga
Rob Daniel
Ellen Durkin
Doug McLean
Vanya Mullinax
Sheldon Sturges
Kathy McGough

and all those countable others who are able to keep
their eyes steadily on the truly important.

Index (abbreviated)

Bibliography & Further Reading

Abbott, E.A., *Flatland, 1884*

Aczel, A.D., *various, 1997 ff*

Aristotle, *various, ca. 360 BCE ff*

Augustine, *various, 386 ff*

Avicenna, *various, ca. 1020 ff*

Barrow, J.D., *The Book of Nothing, 2000*

Boethius, A.M.S., *The Consolation of Philosophy, 525*

The Bible, any version, first written version ca. 800 BCE ff

Chomsky, A.N., *various, 1957 ff*

Collins, F.S., *The Language of God, 2006*

Darwin, C.R., *various, 1839 ff*

Dawkins, R.S., *The God Delusion, 2006; et al. 1976 ff*

Einstein, A., *various, 1905 ff*

Forbes, W.E., *Cycles of Personal Belief, 1917*

Frost, R.L., *various, 1913 ff*

Gould, S.J., *Rocks of Ages, 1999*

Greenblatt, S.J., *The Rise and Fall of Adam and Eve, 2017*

Hawking, S.A., *A Brief History of Time, 1988; et al. 1970 ff*

Hegel, G.W.F., *Phenomenology of Spirit, 1807*

Heisenberg, W.K., *various, 1925 ff*

Huxley, A.L., *various, 1925 ff*

Jung, C.J., *various, ca. 1910 ff*

Lewis, C.S., *Mere Christianity, 1952; et al., ca. 1933 ff*

Nagel, T., *Mind and Cosmos, 2012*

Piaget, J.W.F., *various, 1923 ff*

Pinker, S.A., *The Better Angels of Our Nature, 2011; et al. 2018*

Plato, *Complete Works, 1997; et al. ca. 400 BCE ff*

Randall, L.J., *various, 2005 ff*

Sayers, D.L., *The Lost Tools of Learning, 1947*

Shakespeare, W., *various, ca. 1600*

Tolstoy, L.N., *The Kingdom of God is Within You, 1893; et al.*

Every book written has instruction for the attentive on the matters discussed.

About the Author

Spike Forbes has always lived in Sheridan, Wyoming, enjoying family and grandchildren whenever possible. Just as he shares a birthdate with his grandfather, he has a grandson born on his birthday. He started his schooling in Wyoming, followed by six years at Milton Academy in Massachusetts and Westminster School in London. He attended Yale University, receiving his degree in mathematics in 1964. He taught mathematics for three years serving with the Peace Corps in Honduras, returning for further study at Cornell, Colorado State and Sheridan Community College. Prior to retirement, his working life was in the business of animal agriculture, applying statistical and mathematical theories to biological and economic practice. He has enjoyed active participation on library, school, church, community and national boards. His hobbies include exploration and travel, plus expanded learning and friendships in philosophy, religion, science and agriculture. He is currently an elder with the First Christian Church, Disciples of Christ in Sheridan.